THE ALIVE AND GROWING TEACHER

THE ALIVE AND
GROWING TEACHER

Clark E. Moustakas

The Merrill-Palmer School

Detroit, Michigan

PHILOSOPHICAL LIBRARY
New York

Printed in the United States of America

TO DAVID AND ANNA SMILLIE

teachers who teach by not teaching

ACKNOWLEDGMENTS

I wish to express my appreciation to Dr. Pauline Park Wilson Knapp, Director, and The Merrill-Palmer School for making this publication possible, to David Smillie, Dorothy Lee, and Nancy Samelson, my colleagues, who helped me to think through my experiences in teaching and learning, to Deno Moustakas and Doris Anderson for typing the manuscript in its many transformations, to Betty Moustakas, my wife, whose encouragement and support were always present, and to the many teachers and principals in school systems in Highland Park, Birmingham, Berkley, Ferndale, and Royal Oak, Michigan who contributed much of the raw data and experience upon which the book is based.

Some sections in modified form appeared in a previous publication of the author, Self Explorations of Teachers in a Seminar in Interpersonal Relations, *Journal of Individual Psychology*, 1957, 13, 72-93, and are used here with the permission of the editor, Heinz Ansbacher.

Clark E. Moustakas
June 12, 1958

CONTENTS

PREFACE

THIS book presents a theory of human relatedness and is a portrayal of persons living and learning together. It describes the emotional atmosphere, the conditions and process of learning, and tells what happens to individuals when they are free to be themselves. It is an account of persons struggling with personal and professional issues, problems and concerns, and their growing respect, acceptance, and love for each other. It is a matter of individuals searching for a healthy way to self-fulfillment and fundamental relatedness to others. It presents the experience of a group of persons discovering their own selves' worth-while resources, and through mutual empathy and exchange of ideas coming to the core or essence of their thoughts and feelings.

The particular group involved is a group of classroom teachers and principals but their experience and the underlying theory are relevant to any person concerned with human relations and genuine life with other persons. To present the philosophy apart from a particular group would make it an abstraction without meaning. Yet the personal experiences explored and the nature of the group life are open for others to see whose lives involve similar concerns and struggles. It is certainly a philosophy of teaching but it is also a philosophy of living, of how persons can live together as a group while at the same time recognizing and encouraging the growth of the individual.

The book may serve as a resource through which the individual may come to new awareness of himself as a teacher and as a person. It may enable the individual to contemplate his own beliefs and values and to examine his own relations with others as a way to new pathways of relatedness. It may lead to the creation of insights into educational concepts, issues, practices, and problems. What it will mean in the life of the individual reader will depend on what the reader can bring to it in the way of personal associations and imagery, in what completions and additional clarifications the reader can make for himself.

It is hoped that the book will stimulate further exploratory research into the process of personal growth, the emotional climate required in significant learning, the value of personal inquiry in group experience, the dimensions of human relations, and the nature of teaching and learning.

THE ALIVE AND GROWING TEACHER

CHAPTER 1

GROWTH OF THE SELF

Every experience in which the individual expresses himself in a free, spontaneous manner contributes to the growth of the self. As long as the person maintains the integrity and uniqueness of his individual nature, growth of the self, which begins at birth, continues throughout life. Expression of one's real nature gives substance and strength and enables the person to experience a feeling of freedom and openness which initiates a process of self-education and self-fulfillment.

The urge to express one's individual nature and become fully one's real self lies within each person. This striving has a biological basis and is rooted in the distinct patterning of the human organism. When the urge to actualize one's unique potentials is thwarted the individual is not free to develop in accordance with his own nature. He is closed to many potentially vital and significant experiences. True growth of the person becomes possible when the individual is free to be and to develop and flourish.

The experiences expressed in this volume are essentially an exploration into a structure and process in which teachers may become alive and growing. The story begins with the development of a basic philosophy through which the teacher can come to have faith in himself, believe in his potentialities, and understand the nature of the growth experience. This chapter presents a framework for seeing, sensing, feeling, and knowing the individual in the personal relationship. Within this framework it is possible to create an atmosphere in which teachers can express and explore the nature of their personal and professional experiences, and develop understanding, acceptance, respect, and sensitivity with each other and with human beings everywhere.

The Self

The individual expresses his real self when he is himself alone, a whole person who values his perceptions, and permits himself to flow into life's rich and meaningful experiences. To be one's self is to be alive and unified in the process of life's task—the fulfillment of one's nature and potentiality. There is individuality in each self, stamped in all the component parts of the body and present in the physiological processes as well as in the chemical structure of the human organism (5). The self is an unalterable source and base to which all growth is ultimately ascribed. It strives to realize its potentialities again and again. This striving to develop and actualize, this openness to experience, is constantly present and urges the individual to expression even under the most threatening or defeating circumstances. Because the self is the inside of man, it is that which nothing outside can truly direct or order (38). All that man can do is affect the environment in which a living person can come to his own fulfillment.

The person can never know the self in conscious, defined terms, nor can the self really be classified or categorized. Such knowledge fragments the self until it is nothing at all. The self can be experienced in reflected wholes, in qualities or states of unified feeling and thought in immediate living situations. Only when the individual comes to these awarenesses and feeling-insights through his own self-discovery is a real discovery made (3).

Though expression of self means uniqueness it also includes universality. The self is a unitary source of diverse, bodily expressed insistencies and of a single concern for an all-embracing good (38). It is the center of a universal concern for the fulfillment of human potential everywhere. The self contains the forces which set the body into action, and move the individual forward to ordered and complete development. It is the integration or unity of the person's intrinsic nature, and his being and becoming in life's significant experience.

Intrinsic Nature and Individuality

Every person is born a unique individual and remains so throughout his life. Even when the development of personality has been thwarted and the potentialities of the self are unfulfilled, a certain core or quality intrinsic to one's inner nature persists and stamps a mark of individuality on the person. The irrevocable biological basis of individuality has been described by the surgeon, Alexis Carrel (5, p. 267) as follows:

"Individual specificity persists during the entire life, although tissues and humors continually change. The organs and their medium move at the rhythm of physiological time, that is, at the rhythm of irreversible processes, towards definitive transformations and death. But they always keep their inherent qualities."

Based on exhaustive studies of the nature of organs, tissues, and cells in higher organisms, Loeb (22, p. 4) arrived at a similar conclusion:

"There are *properties* which are not restricted to certain parts of the organism, but which are *common to all, or almost all, parts of the organism,* and which, although not visible, bind them together, make them into a unit and differentiate one individual from every other individual. . . . There is inherent in every higher individual organism something which differentiates him from every other individual, which can be discovered by observing the reactions of certain cells and tissues belonging to one individual towards the tissues and cells of another individual of the same species."

In all the transformations of the individual, biological and otherwise, certain persistent characteristics remain. These inherent qualities of the organism are the potential basis for creative expression and original behavior. The individual is born with personal integrity which can be stifled and weakened but never completely destroyed. To the extent that this intrinsic nature of the individual is honored, nourished and cultivated, the person maintains his integrity. The intrinsic qualities become more distinct and lead to originality of attitude in all significant or crucial human endeavors. Though unseen, the intrinsic nature of each individual affects the nature of his growth and development.

Being

Being is the boundary and structure of individual life. For a person to be, there is one basic requirement, that the individual be true to himself. Only in true expression of one's own being can growth occur. Thus being is an essential condition to growth or becoming.

Being is the experience of oneself as a totality, as a whole, in the immediate presence. In the being experience there is no sense of time or direction, or separation of self from other. There is a complete absorption, self-involvement, and fullness. One cannot plan to be. One can only plan to be about to be. An experience of being is spontaneous and simply happens, comes, or grows within significant personal situations. Only when one does not plan to listen to learn is one fully open to experience. Listening to learn may lead to partial and temporary achievements but full presence of being includes listening and enables the individual to develop in every way he can.

In her childhood, Mrs. Lawrence, a fifth grade teacher, was permitted to listen to music only for certain definite purposes. Her musical experiences were controlled by her parents. They selected the instruments she was required to learn to play. They took her to concerts and symphonies they felt would contribute to her knowledge and skill and urged her to listen for variations in theme, tone, and pitch. She was not permitted to listen to music on the radio or on records as this was felt to be a second-hand approach. They wanted her to have only the authentic experience of fresh music not recorded material. In spite of all the special experiences they arranged for her, Mrs. Lawrence was unable to distinguish differences in tone. She deceived her parents and teachers because she could play mechanically with superior skill. Then in college, for the first time she had an opportunity to be alone and to listen to symphonies on her own and in her own room. Here there was no purpose in listening to the music, no knowledge to be gained or questions to answer. Basically, there was the opportunity to be and to experience the organic unity of the symphony. It was sometime later, in a situation requiring Mrs. Lawrence to recognize variations in tone and pitch, that she realized that she actually could feel these differences. Through the being experience in music, she had learned to distinguish differences in sound, not mechanically and out of abstract knowledge, but in feeling and experiencing these variations.

Being is the form, pattern, or context of individuality. It is the basis or guide which determines the nature of the development of a particular person.

Though a necessary condition to growth, being is good only as itself. Being is complete in itself and does not necessarily lead to changes in development. Being exists in the individual's absorption in an activity where there is sheer satisfaction in perceiving, contemplating, sensing, listening, and expressing, a complete experience. Being cannot be understood as changing, or by relating one being to others, or from cause-effect analyses but only as a substantial core of a unified totality, the self.

Being is good and true in terms of pattern (19). Pattern is the guide. As Paul Weiss (38, p. 267) states it: "Man is a natural being with a fixed core, directed towards a good which is pertinent to all that exists. He has infinite value because he has infinite responsibility."

Self-Actualization, Becoming, Growth

While being is the consistent core, the immutable structure of the individual, becoming refers to the person as a process. Several terms are used here to convey a similar theme, the emerging, unfolding expressions of the individual's potentialities. As stated earlier, it is the basic tendency of the individual to become himself, to develop his capacities in accordance with his own nature. This process of becoming continues throughout the life of the human organism, and remains a constant urge. Karen Horney (15, p. 17) has stated the principle briefly: "The human individual, given a chance, tends to develop his particular human potentialities." This urging of the individual to grow is not a passive state waiting to be stimulated or energized from the outside. It is not a quiescent drive which must be activated by external pressures and external attempts to motivate. It is not an effort to relieve the organism of tensions. On the contrary the urge to become is a force positively present. It is the nature of the organism to strive toward its own development, to move in a forward direction. Even if we wished it differently, only the organism can actualize its potentialities. It must do its own learning and it must do its own growing.

The process of becoming determines what is real for the person (35). Within this process the individual increasingly discovers his sources of strength and his integrity. Becoming a person means exploring the nature of one's experience, sensing one's development, organizing and unifying feeling and thought into meaningful patterns of behavior. Rollo May (26) has emphasized that this means not only learning to feel, to experience, and to want, but to fight against what prevents the person from feeling and wanting.

Self-awareness is involved in the process of becoming. Allport (1) says the process of becoming is a matter of organizing transitory impulses into a pattern of striving and interest in which the element of self-awareness plays a part. But this awareness is not always a conscious, deliberate, or cognitive experience. Often self-awareness exists in the form of intuitive knowing, a sense of rightness and congruity, a gestalt, or in inner communion.

Change and learning do not necessarily lead to growth or becoming. The individual may learn ideas and feelings external to intrinsic nature and being. Though learnings may result in continuous and apparently permanent changes in behavior when external to the self they are not expressions of real growth. Only changes which are consistent with the self, which have to do with the actualizing of one's potentials, are true indications of growth or becoming.

True or Significant Experience

Not all experience leads to growth. Experience must relate to one's potentialities and individuality, be consistent with what one wants to do, must involve the real person before it can be true or significant. It must touch the person in his being and in his course of becoming. In this kind of experience intrinsic nature, being, and becoming merge and unify into the self. When the real self is expressed and explored, it changes in quality or state, moving toward higher integration of cognitive and conative processes.

John Dewey emphasized that there is only one permanent frame of reference; namely, the organic connection between education and personal experience (7). Without the personal self in experience, there can be no real growth. It is *we* who emerge in experiencing and what we emerge into in experiencing the meaning of something is the truth about that thing.

True experience begins with the person as he truly is and ends with the person having unique perceptions, new insights, meanings, and feelings. External controls must be rejected as they are outside experience. The problem then is to find these factors of control that are inherent within experience (7). This is not a real problem, however, as long as individuals are free to be themselves, since the structure or boundary or control lies in the intrinsic nature of the individual and in his state of being and is expressed naturally when the self is nourished and loved.

True experience is always immanent to the immediate situation in which the individual is. This does not mean that the individual is conscious of his state of being and his striving to grow, or even of his interests or purposes. John Dewey has pointed out that what is not explicitly present makes up a vastly greater part of experience than does the conscious field to which thinkers have so devoted themselves. Experience is something quite other than consciousness (8). There is something immediate and non-cognitively present in true or significant experience so that it must be pointed to rather than explained, defined or categorized. If the person is acting on expectations or values of others, if he acts to please or be approved of, if he does anything which violates his own nature or integrity, there can be no true or significant experience.

Summarizing Comments

The self cannot really be defined. To define it is to make it what it is not. It has universal qualities yet it exists uniquely in each individual. The self as a concept is only words, as are intrinsic nature, being, and becoming, theoretical constructs which as constructs cannot be perceived, felt, known, or even understood. Only in true or significant experience does the self become a reality. Such experience must touch the core of one's being and contain an underlying unity and distinctiveness. It must be immanent or immediate. It must involve expressions of the self which unify or integrate one's intrinsic nature with an immediate state of being and a process of becoming or growth.

Man's physical and mental life reaches into a nourishing and embracing power that he senses and that works in him though it is beyond his intellectual grasp (37). Even in true experience, the self, because of its complexity and breadth, cannot be fully known but its qualities or states can be felt and perceived as reflections of an inconceivable totality or whole.

Expressions of the Real Self

Expressions of the real self reflect the natural emergence of potentiality. They are unified and consistent in behavior, not the wild, confused and fragmentary "acting out" often designated as self-expression. This kind of self-expression is externally motivated, a reaction to frustration, denial, and rejection, to not being a self. To be, an expression of the self must honor the individuality of personality but must also be an all-embracing good, a provision for the realization of goodness in others. As Niebuhr has stated: "There is no point at which the self, seeking its own, can feel itself self-satisfied and free to consider others than itself. The con-

cern for others is as immediate as the concern for itself"
(29, p. 139). Respect for one's own integrity and uniqueness, love for and understanding of one's own self, cannot
be separated from respect for and love and understanding
of another individual (11). The creative expression of the
self is always constructive (31).

Two quotations refer to the misunderstanding and confusion which arise when self-expression becomes an educational issue and its essential meaning and character are not
understood. In an important book (26, p. 56) Rollo May
wrote:

"Those of us who lived in the 1920's can recall the evi-
dences of the growing tendency to think of the self in
superficial and oversimplified terms. In those days 'self-
expression' was supposed to be simply doing whatever
popped into one's head, as though the self were synonymous
with any random impulse, and as though one's decisions
were to be made on the basis of a whim which might be a
product of digestion from a hurried lunch just as often as
one's philosophy of life. To 'be yourself' was then an excuse to relaxing into the lowest common denominator of
inclination. To 'know one's self' wasn't thought to be especially different and the problems of personality could be
solved relatively easily by better 'adjustment.'"

Recently Rasey and Menge (32, p. 56) comment on the
same confusion:

"Charges often brought against the so-called new education are phrased in such fashion as: 'So you want him to
do just as he pleases? Whatever he wants he must have!'
These criticisms must be met with the obvious fact that it
is not what *we* want, it is a question of the way the organism operates. It is a fact of human construction, not a matter of educational philosophy."

If real expression of the self can be a bad thing, the
blame lies not with the self but with the universe, with
providence (9). Unless the self is free to express itself, to

react with uniqueness and distinctiveness in every situation which is significant, meaningful, and a challenge to one's potentialities, the very capacity for growth is stifled and denied. Expression of the self is the individual's way of asserting his own yes-feeling, emerging from his own root system (14).

Desire is a forward urge of living creatures. It is activity surging forward to break through what dams it up (9). To desire is to want, to feel, to be free to choose. The person must know what he wants, not always consciously but spontaneously and uniquely in experience. Knowing what one wants is simply the elemental form of what in the maturing person is the ability to choose one's own values (26).

As long as a situation has an immediate appeal to the real self, it is not necessary to ask what it is good for. As John Dewey has indicated (6, p. 283) "This is a question which can be asked only about instrumental values, but some goods are not good *for* anything; they are just goods. Any other notion leads to an absurdity."

Wanting is not the blind and capricious impulse that sometimes is associated with it but rather the necessary feeling or urge that makes vital experience and true growth possible. Wanting includes the rational, logical, and cognitive just as it incorporates the feeling-aspects of experience. Thought is included not as reflection or separated contemplation but rather as a unity, a oneness of thought and feeling, of feeling and understanding in true and significant experience. Without this unity there can be no personal meaning or sense. The intellectual anticipation, the significant idea or concept must blend with desire and impulse to acquire moving force (6). Sometimes this unity is referred to as intuitive knowing or intuitive insight and occurs as a unified expression of the self. It appears as a vision, a deeper unity of dispersed entities and is a feeling of being *with-in* the situation, object, or other person and not before or outside of it (37).

One further differentiation must be denoted here, the difference between wanting and needing. Wanting is an affirmative expression of the self related to something of intrinsic worth to the individual while needing often refers to lacks and gaps which the individual should fill or for which he must compensate. Only the person in his individuality and in the totality of his significant experience can know what he wants but others know what he needs. Wanting involves being and choosing but needing often means following a prescribed path and a predetermined goal to make up for deficits.

A quality of the real self is wanting in terms of positive growth, not needing in terms of absences and weaknesses. Wanting is an experience of growing in the total organism while needing often relates to satiation of specific drives. Wanting is a unique positive self-fulfilling force consistent with the unity of the self, not a need for norms or standards. Maslow (23, p. 24) explains some of these differences between wanting and needing in terms of deficiency motivation and growth motivation. He describes how the individual feels when he is constantly *needed:*

"We may not be aware when *we* perceive in a need-determined way. But we certainly are aware of it when *we* ourselves are perceived in this way, e.g., simply as a money-giver, a food-supplier, a safety-giver, someone to depend on, or as a waiter or other anonymous servant or means-object. When this happens we don't like it at all. We want to be taken for ourselves, as complete and whole individuals. We dislike being perceived as useful objects or as tools. We dislike being 'used.' "

To express one's self in true or significant experience is a positive and affirmative act in realizing potentialities, in becoming increasingly self-educated. The self by its nature is inclined to grow and has the capacity to unify thought and feeling in action into more meaningful and more inclusive wholes.

Freedom and Responsibility

The individual cannot grow in accordance with his own nature unless he is free, both within himself and in his relations with others. To be free is to accept oneself in totality, to respect one's individuality, and to be open and ready to grow in all of life's significant experiences. Freedom naturally means the selection of human values which foster growth. John Dewey says that freedom contains three elements of importance: (1) efficiency in action and the absence of cramping and thwarting obstacles, (2) capacity to change the course of action and to experience novelties and (3) the power of desire and choice to be factors in events (9). Freedom includes a basic attitude of allowing one's own self to be the guiding force in all significant experience, to allow one's self to discover truth, and to express truth as one sees it.

There can be no freedom without responsibility. This does not become an issue unless one deals with sick people who have become sick as the self has been denied and blocked in its expression. Self-discipline, self-criticism, and self-responsibility are inherent tendencies in the organism (3). The self is the responsible, innermost core of man; it is the ultimate source of all his acts. To be positively free is to be simultaneously spontaneous and thoughtful, self-enhancing and other-enhancing, self-valuing and valuing of others, accepting and responsible.

Unity

Another quality of the real self is unity. The element of unity or wholeness is reflected in every living situation. When the individual becomes a real person there is integrity and unity in his experience. There is fullness and variety. Unity itself, unity of the person, unity of the life lived must be emphasized again and again. Only in this personal unity can a unity of mankind be born (4).

Unity can be seen in the biological make-up of man. From exhaustive studies of the biological processes in higher organisms, Loeb reports that the bodily mechanism of the more complex organisms is unified into individual wholes by the individuality differentials, the nervous system, and the hormones carried by the circulating fluids in each unique organism (22). The organism is born in unity and to unify. This unity must be maintained or the uniqueness and integrity of the organism, the organism itself, becomes diseased and decays. The necessity of maintaining the unity of the system is a universal dynamic principle, intrinsic to the nature of the organism. *Not conflict but unity is the fundamental postulate* (18). Without this unity of the self or persistence of pattern in life, without the integration of intrinsic nature, and being and becoming into meaningful wholes in vital experience there can be no self, only conflict and inconsistency.

The unifying pattern of self makes the real person a whole person. The unity integrates thought and feeling and gives coherence to everything the individual does (10).

Unity or wholeness of the person can be known in the empathy and love of significant personal relationships, in communion, and in spontaneous, immediate, significant personal encounters. The unity itself, the harmony of one's own life seems to come from an increasing capacity to find in the world that which also obtains within the depths of one's own being (27).

References

1. Allport, Gordon. *Becoming.* New Haven: Yale University Press, 1955.
2. Angyal, Andras. *Foundations for a Science of Personality.* New York: The Commonwealth Fund, 1941.

3. Brctall, Robert (Ed.) *A Kierkegaard Anthology.* Princeton, 1946.
4. Buber, Martin (Tr. by Ronald Gregor Smith). *Between Man and Man.* Boston: Beacon Press, 1955.
5. Carrel, Alexis. *Man the Unknown.* New York: Harper & Brothers Publishers, 1935.
6. Dewey, John. *Democracy and Education.* New York: The MacMillan Company, 1916.
7. Dcwcy, John. *Experience and Education.* New York: The MacMillan Company, 1938.
8. Dewey, John. *Experience and Nature.* Chicago: Open Court Publishing Company, 1925.
9. Dewey, John. *Human Nature and Conduct.* New York: Henry Holt and Company, 1922.
10. Fosdick, Harry Emerson. *On Being a Real Person.* New York: Harper & Brothers, 1943.
11. Fromm, Erich. *Man for Himself: An Inquiry Into the Psychology of Ethics.* New York: Rinehart & Company, Inc., 1947.
12. Goldstein, Kurt. The Concept of Health, Disease, and Therapy. *Amer. J. Psychiat.,* 1954, 8, 745-764.
13. Goldstein, Kurt. *The Organism.* New York: American Book Co., 1939.
14. Horney, Karen. Finding the Real Self. *Amer. J. Psychiat.,* Vol. IX, 1949.
15. Horney, Karen. *Neurosis and Human Growth.* New York: W. W. Norton & Co., Inc., 1950.
16. Jung, C. G. *The Integration of the Personality.* London: Routledge & Kegan Paul, 1950.
17. Kelley, Earl C. *Education for What is Real.* New York: Harper & Brothers, 1947.
18. Lecky, Prescott. Frederick G. Thorne (Ed.). *Self-Consistency: A Theory of Personality.* New York: Island Press Co-operative, Inc., 1951.
19. Lee, Dorothy. Being and Value in A Primitive Culture. *J. Phil.,* 1949, 46, (13), 401-415.

20. Lee, Dorothy. The Joy of Work as Participation. In *The Hour of Insight* ed. by R. M. MacIver. New York: Harper & Brothers, 1954.

21. Lee, Dorothy. Lineal and Nonlineal Codifications of Reality. *Psychosomatic Medicine,* Vol. XII, Number 2, 89-97, March-April, 1950.

22. Loeb, Leo. *The Biological Basis of Individuality.* Springfield, Illinois: Charles C. Thomas, 1945.

23. Maslow, Abraham. Deficiency Motivation and Growth Motivation. Ed. by Marshall R. Jones. *Nebraska Symposium on Motivation.* Lincoln: University of Nebraska Press, 1955.

24. Maslow, A. H. The Instinctoid Nature of Basic Needs. *J. Pers.,* 1954, 22, 326-347.

25. Maslow, A. H. *Motivation and Personality.* New York: Harper & Brothers, 1954.

26. May, Rollo. *Man's Search for Himself.* New York: W. W. Norton & Company, 1953.

27. Mooney, Ross L. Creation, Parents, and Children. *Prog. Educ.,* 1953, 31, 14-17.

28. Moustakas, Clark E. (Ed.). *The Self.* New York: Harper & Brothers, 1956.

29. Niebuhr, Reinhold. *The Self and the Dramas of History.* New York: Charles Scribner's Sons, 1955.

30. Rank, Otto. *Modern Education.* New York: Alfred A. Knopf, Inc., 1932.

31. Rank, Otto. *Will Therapy and Truth and Reality.* New York: Alfred A. Knopf, 1950.

32. Rasey, Marie, and Menge, J. W. *What We Learn from Children.* New York: Harper & Brothers, 1956.

33. Rogers, Carl R. *Client-Centered Therapy.* Boston: Houghton Mifflin Company, 1951.

34. Sinnott, Edmund W. *The Biology of the Spirit.* New York: The Viking Press, 1955.

35. Smillie, David. Truth and Reality from Two Points of

View in *The Self,* ed. by Clark E. Moustakas. New York: Harper & Brothers, 1956.

36. Tillich, Paul. *The Courage To Be.* New Haven: Yale University Press, 1952.

37. Ulich, Robert. *The Human Career:* A Philosophy of Self-Transcendence. New York: Harper & Brothers, 1955.

38. Weiss, Paul. *Nature and Man.* New York: Henry Holt & Co., 1947.

CHAPTER 2

THE PROCESS OF PERSONAL GROWTH

Theories of human nature and behavior are abstractions which come to life in the concrete reality of the learner in the immediate situation. They must be in the self and expressions of the self to be significant to the learner.

Growth in a group of learners depends upon the kind of atmosphere which is initially created by the teacher or nurturer. Eventually each individual in the group helps to determine whether real expressions of the self and self-exploration will exist or whether fear, need for praise and approval, repetition, stereotype, and adherence to external standards will prevail.

The Behavior of the Teacher

The teacher must be responsible initially for conveying the nature and essence of his philosophy and for creating an accepting, non-judgmental atmosphere where each individual is valued as a person. His presentation is a way of pointing to or denoting the essential values and meanings of a theory of health and growth. He must express himself with feeling and conviction for only if he experiences with his entire being what he says can he help to create a learning experience for another or even to initiate a process by which a growth experience can occur. The teacher expresses his experience as his own, in a personal approach, not as something objectified or impersonal. He must not impose himself on the learner but, on the contrary, must encourage the learner to evolve his own values and convictions with greater clarity and to develop insights consistent with his own experience. He must regard the many questions and reactions of the learner with utter respect, listening with complete acceptance and making elaborations where this is important to the learner. He must allow the learner's point of view to emerge, be treated with respect, and valued. During the initial meetings an atmosphere of mutual acceptance, trust, and love must develop which helps free the individual participants, including the teacher. The teacher, with his whole being, actively encourages each individual to be and become more fully himself. He recognizes the individual perceptions of each person as worthy. He attempts to nurture and cultivate the learner's ideas and shows his belief in the dynamic value and social significance of the learner's experience.

The beginning is made by the teacher, never as an authority, but as a person concerned with the becoming nature of each member in the group and with his own personal growth. He starts with his philosophy, his convictions, his attitudes, not with a definition of his function or role. Definition is just another form of authority. It means "to end off." As has been observed by Cantor, the time for definition is at the end of exploration not at the beginning (2). And when an exploration ends, definitions are no longer important.

The teacher does not begin with hypotheses about learners for this makes belief in growth tentative, and suggests doubt. He must have firm faith in the potentiality of the learner. If he fails, it means that a true occasion for learning failed to emerge. To doubt the validity of one's belief in the person, of one's value of the person, is not to believe or value at all. Only when the instructor is present in the full human sense, not hypothetically but truly, is he able to grow as a unified totality and thus provide an occasion for the growth of others.

With each group the teacher begins in a new way for he is a learner too, concerned with his own being and growth. Every person he encounters in his teachings constitutes a new experience and a new opportunity for development. He does not function in any predesignated or predetermined fashion. He expresses himself spontaneously, intuitively and in terms of the immediate situation as he sees it. Buber (1, p. 114) has emphasized this value, as follows: "In spite of all similarities, every living situation has, like a newborn child, a new face that has never been before and will never come again. It demands of you a reaction which cannot be prepared beforehand. It demands nothing of what is past. It demands presence, responsibility; it demands you."

The teacher must satisfy situations out of deep readiness to respond with his whole being and in such a way that his actions and attitudes express the unity of his being and his willingness to accept responsibility. Once the initial "pointing to" is completed, the teacher must listen to each person fully so that he may experience for himself the essence of the learner's expression. As a listener, the teacher, at first, sometimes hears only the surface expressions but soon the wonder of the real person begins to emerge. The teacher listens to understand but he listens also to learn for himself from the experiences of others. He encourages individual learners to maintain positions they feel are right and valid. He encourages them to further express and explore in a free and natural manner the nature of their own experience. He regards expression of self as the key to self-education. He believes that expressing real experience is often a necessary aspect of the process of growth, in clarifying and resolving issues, in seeing new possibilities in life situations, in emerging with hope from despair and failure, in changing one's feelings and ideas, in developing positive personal relations.

In a very important sense, the expression of a vital experience is itself a continuation of experience (3). The person is not simply reporting, or repeating, not just talking about or re-making something which has occurred but rather is, in the very act of expressing, creating for himself and others new images, perceptions, and insights. He is exploring in a vital sense and these expressions of self when open and free lead to personal values, meanings, and discoveries. In the act of expressing, the self of the learner comes to birth. Niblett (3, p. 115) quotes from A. Cluttonbrock, the essayist, in describing the creative nature of expressions of the self:

"If I try to say something exactly, I am not trying to say what I have to say already. I am trying to make myself in saying it. When Beethoven thought a symphony, he was not writing down something which had already stamped itself on his mind. He was making himself as well as the symphony, becoming more and more precisely Beethoven as he achieved a more and more precise expression of Beethoven."

The teacher not only listens but also expresses his point of view from time to time. When he does so, however, it is an expression of the self, an utterance, a pointing to, or an exploration of his own self-experience, never an imposition, never to make others feel that they should think as he does. On the contrary, because he may have a special status in the eyes of learners and may contribute superficially or falsely to the learning process, he deliberately and consciously encourages others to express and maintain their own perceptions and convictions. He knows significant growth occurs from expressions of real experience not from repetitions of authoritative statements or strivings for approval.

There are times in living with the group when the teacher directly supports individual members who are being attacked or whose integrity and self-respect are being threatened. In supporting an individual, the teacher must not attack or minimize or deny the feelings of others in the group. He expresses himself because he wants the individual to know he recognizes and values him and because he wants the individual to feel he is not entirely alone in the world.

The teacher knows, not as rationalized thought, but within experience that when the self of a learner is threatened the process of growth is stifled. The errors of the individual learner, his misgivings and inadequacies, his distortions, are things he can discover only for himself. It is only when he discovers them that a discovery is made even though the whole group thinks it knows the answers and the sources of error beforehand. The process of growth is stopped when answers are given, when aspects of a totality are analyzed, when accusations are made, when the creative act of expression and exploration is blocked.

The teacher must encourage learners to experiment and try out ideas that occur to them through their own self-explorations. He must actively show his belief in the worth and dignity of each individual in the group, his regard for their potentialities as creative persons. He must convey attitudes of acceptance and empathy in response to the expressions of learners.

The process of growth in a group of learners proceeds as follows: The teacher initially expresses his theory of the self, self-being and growth, together with the concrete principles that relate to it. This provides a structure and points to a basis for understanding and valuing the essence of the human person as a learner. It initiates an atmosphere of spontaneity and freedom in which trust, acceptance, and respect develop as basic self-attitudes. This begins the process of self-exploration in which each member of the group participates. As the person explores his experience new images emerge, and unified and complete insights appear, not only for the individual expressing himself but also for those individuals who are truly able to experience and integrate into their own lives the experience of another person. There is a merging of the professional activities of the teacher with his total life situation. The teacher is alive in the fullest sense, a being with self-consistency and structure, but also fully growing and becoming.

References

1. Buber, Martin. *Between Man and Man.* Tr. by Ronald Gregor Smith. Boston: Beacon Press, 1955.
2. Cantor, Nathaniel. *The Teaching-Learning Process.* New York: Dryden Press, 1953.
3. Niblett, W. R. *Education—The Lost Dimension.* New York: William Sloan Associates, Inc., 1955.

CHAPTER 3

THE TEACHER'S EXPRESSION OF SELF
IN RELATIONS WITH OTHER TEACHERS

Experiences with other teachers have an important bearing on the teacher's behavior not only in the classroom but in all significant relations. These experiences can be strengthening occasions for learning and personal growth or they can be critical, rejecting and bitter. They can promote a sense of well-being and trust which frees the teacher to be spontaneous and creative in the school or they can arouse anxieties and feelings of inadequacy. Relations with other teachers and administrators can help the teacher maintain his integrity as a unified, whole person or they can divide the teacher and force him to play roles, to act a part and to please and pacify others, rather than to be himself and value his own being.

Understanding of others often begins with self-exploration and self-insight. In 1919 in his talks to teachers, William James (3, p. 3) wrote:

"In whatever sphere of education their functions may lie, there is to be seen among them a really inspiring amount of searching of the heart about the highest concerns of their profession. . . . The teachers of this country, one may say, have its future in their hands. The earnestness which they at present show in striving to enlighten and strengthen themselves is an index of the nation's probabilities of advance in all ideal directions."

This attitude of teachers exists today. Search for clarity, self-discovery and professional insight characterize teachers when they have the freedom to explore and grow, when there is recognition and valuing of their own vital and dynamic experience as the source of further growth and development. Self-searching occurs in an atmosphere of affection where the terrors of loneliness are assuaged and the impulse freely to link hands with others is strengthened (1).

There is no way to force the teacher to learn and to grow. He must want to express his potentialities and to explore his experiences from personal choice and value. Only then can self-exploration be a process, a vital experience itself, and not a reporting, summing up or analysis. The urge to develop and grow is within each individual. The striving for different levels of meaning and knowledge can be recognized in another person, pointed to, and valued but it cannot be "drawn out," tricked into activation, or manipulated. The teacher will learn significantly only those things which *are* involved in the growth of the self. Any other type of learning is temporary and disappears when threats are removed, or persists in a context of personal anxiety.

The teacher can be deliberately encouraged to feel for himself, think, for himself, be himself but not through external rewards or motives. Too often external motives are used to trap attention and coerce effort to get individuals to engage in projects which have necessarily no intrinsic worth to command the person's interest (5).

In the classroom situation, both teacher and learner have potentialities for growth. These potentialities are free to come to expression and be actualized when the teacher is a learner and the learner, without knowing it, is a teacher. On the whole, the less consciousness there is, on either side, of either giving or receiving instruction, the better (2).

Self-References in A Group of Classroom Teachers

Teachers feel free to express the nature of their experience and to openly explore personal relations when a feeling of mutual confidence and trust exists in the group. Often, in the beginning, there is some anxiety in individual members as to whether it is safe to relate personal feelings and thoughts in the group. Many questions arise: Can members of the group really trust each other? Would teachers' personal expressions be repeated outside the group? Is it not safer to keep bad experiences to one's self? An open exploration of these questions frees the teacher to look into the nature of his relations with other teachers and with administrators.

The excerpt below illustrates the anxiety felt in a group after two teachers had expressed the nature of their negative relations with parents and principals. The two teachers had disagreed strongly on how to bring about a change in these relations.

Mr. Frank: You did a beautiful job of doing what I was saying we should do. I've known people just full of things to say and they just barely get out a sentence or two when someone interrupts. I'm guilty of that. You didn't interrupt each other at all. You each waited until the other had said all he wanted to. I've been watching this discussion very carefully. Did you feel you understood each other?

Mrs. Sall: Yes, and I felt accepted.

Mr. James: But other people didn't react to you.

Mrs. Sall: I felt acceptance even though no one said anything directly.

Mr. James: Didn't you feel you were putting yourself on the carpet?

Mrs. Sall: No.

Mr. James: Now I didn't have that feeling. When you were talking about administrators, I felt the silence in the group intimated, "Don't talk. Don't be a fool." That's the feeling I got.

Mrs. Dase: Because you are afraid that what we say here will get back.

Mr. James: I don't say that's the way we all feel but perhaps we've all had experiences where something we've said is brought back to us. It might have been repeated unconsciously. So we feel in here we have to be careful about what we say.

Mr. Wann: People easily misquote and misinterpret one another.

Mrs. Long: If that's true, somewhere along the line we've failed. I have felt we could say anything here without fear that reference would be made outside. This is the first indication I have had of someone withholding.

Mrs. Sall: Some of the friends I have hold a cynical attitude toward this group. They've tried hard to find out what we discuss here and each time they run into a blank wall.

Mr. James: I'm saying that at an unguarded moment someone may make a remark which gives others the wrong idea and someone may be hurt. Even though I trust all of you implicitly, I wouldn't tell you all I know.

Mrs. Dase: Yes but we're here for just that reason, to say what's in our hearts and minds. If we can't do that, there's no point in being here.

Mrs. Long: Yes, that's why I consider this experience so unusual, so worthwhile.

Mr. Frank: Would you tell this group the worst thing that ever happened to you in teaching?

Mrs. Long: Yes, I would without even wondering about it, until now.

Mrs. Wull: If we are secure enough, it won't matter if we are misinterpreted. It is much more important to feel the acceptance and trust of the group.

Mr. James: But when you are misinterpreted, it hurts.

Mrs. Dase: I can understand why you say that. Someone has hurt you, gotten back at you.

Miss Whet: My father was a minister. When you grow up in a family like that, you just don't talk. You just don't. If you do, you're in hot water. I don't care who the group is.

Mr. Frank: Right now you are talking about how you feel, expressing yourself and taking us into your trusted confidence.

Mrs. Allen: I agree that what we say here shouldn't bring harm to anyone.

Mrs. Dase: If you say something that brings harm to someone then it's gossip.

Mrs. Sall: But teachers do it all the time. We don't have the courage to tell the person what we think.

Mrs. Walk: If we really believe in something and say so, we are better equipped for teaching than we are if we do it because someone else says so or because someone else does it.

Mrs. Wull: You were sincere that day you told us about the difficulty you had with noise.

Mrs. Walk: Yes, I felt it and I wanted all of you to know. I'm not proud of some things I've done with children but I just couldn't go on year after year subjecting 30 children to a program I couldn't believe in. I hated it. I hated it morning and night.

Mrs. Long: You were sincere to feel it yourself and to say how you felt. There are others who have felt as you did, but couldn't say it.

Mrs. Sall: Everyone here can express how he feels. We don't have to mention certain facts or people's names or places.

Comments

The basic issue in the discussion is clear: Can the individual feel safe in expressing his feelings and know that he will not be quoted outside the group? A few teachers express their reluctance and doubt but as the discussion proceeds, there seems to be a consensus of feeling in the group that without confidence, spontaneity, and freedom, the meetings cannot be real experiences. Discussion of doubt and distrust seem necessary for some individuals in the group. They open the way for reinforcement of the positive values and attitudes initially expressed by the instructor and later by other members of the group. Mr. James and Miss Whet who were the most questioning and most concerned, the most distrustful in the initial meetings, later brought into the group many personal experiences and freely explored the nature of their problems and relations with others, expressing their beliefs and attitudes on vital issues with a feeling of safety and confidence. Apparently being able to express distrust in an accepting atmosphere, makes it possible for the individual to come to be trusting.

Teachers' Rejection of Each Other

When the individual is taught to imitate others, when he is urged to compensate for lacks or treated according to what others think he needs or should have, the inherent growth strivings and tendency to realize one's potentialities are blocked. If the individual is rejected, criticized, or attacked, he often becomes static or defensive rather than exploratory and actualizing.

Praise or reward and punishment work in similar ways to prevent the learner from really growing. These methods of influencing the learner help to create a feeling of disrespect and a judgmental atmosphere which put the learner under scrutiny. When the learner is being judged, whether positively or negatively, he is unfree to express his real self.

When one acts to gain another's praise or to avoid punishment, the act itself is a living reminder of the feeling of weakness and worthlessness; acting to please others undermines courage (4). Both satisfaction and pain are intrinsic to true experience, and, unseparated from the self, become attributes of a totality in experience. That education is literally and all the time its own reward means that every study or discipline is worthwhile in its own immediate having (2).

Sometimes an experience of rejection in school has a strong impact on the teacher's life outside school. Mrs. Walk, in the following excerpt, expresses the nature of her unhappy life in school and finds support and strength from the group. She emerges with a special kind of courage and a determination to continue to strive for health and goodness in her relations with other teachers, even when she is criticized and rejected by them.

Mrs. Walk: The first time in a long time that I sat down in class and considerably enjoyed myself. I felt peaceful and that's a very unusual feeling because I haven't been feeling that way. Of course, it didn't last long—only one day. Then Mr. Frank and Dr. Howard came over. They came into my room, just to visit. I would like to tell about that.

Mr. Frank: When we stepped into Virginia's room her first remark was, "I'm being a very strict teacher today." The children were sitting very quietly. They were having an arithmetic lesson. They were being taught simple addition by a very unique method. The thing I noticed mostly the kids seemed to enjoy not knowing how to do it. Each time Mrs. Walk asked "How many do not understand?" about three-fourths of the room had their hands up. Then she'd ask, "Now who would like to explain it," and the same three-fourths put their hands up. They seemed to be making a game of it but it was a very well-behaved group of kids. I observed them later on the playground. They seemed to be a very normal, lively bunch of kids tearing around and fighting. I got the feeling that things were not in a turmoil, not so bad as Mrs. Walk has reported.

Mrs. Walk: The day Mr. Frank came in I had decided to be a strict teacher and I didn't enjoy it. I didn't enjoy seeing myself be that kind of teacher.

Mr. Frank: Well, one thing that impressed me, the kids didn't seem to object. You set limits but they accepted them.

Mrs. Long: Possibly they rebelled by pretending not to understand what Mrs. Walk was teaching them.

Mr. Frank: I sensed you were uncomfortable. They were getting you down and you didn't like it.

Mrs. Walk: I find children frequently say they do not understand when they do. After you left, things got bad. I stuck my neck out. I put a note on the bulletin board asking that the teachers who were complaining about the noise come and tell me about it instead of going to the principal. I started the note in a very negative way, not meaning to. It angered one of the teachers who pounced on me. She harped at me how I unconsciously was trying to hurt some teachers in the building, but it was a pattern I had set up in my life—digging at others and wanting to hurt them. She completely—I couldn't—I felt so completely broken down.

Mrs. Long: Why did the note anger her so?

Mrs. Walk: It—it started her on me. She told me she was telling me everything she had felt about me for a long time. Things she said she could not have said earlier.

Mrs. Dase: She picked a good time when you were having so much trouble with the children.

Mrs. Walk: She was honest but it hurt me badly. Her criticisms and what she said all the others in the building thought about me, that I was unfit to be a teacher.

Mrs. Dase: Sometimes I wonder what kind of a profession we have. We go around with such an air of dignity and then destroy the sense of value and the integrity of a fellow teacher.

Mrs. Sall: It's happened to many of us. One of my colleagues told a member of the Board of Education that I was an unfit person to teach. The superintendent called me into his office. He was inclined to be emotional at times. He told me one of the board members had asked him if I were fit to be a teacher. I was shocked. When the story came out I learned that one of the teachers had reported that I took young children off the street to care for them but locked them out of my house. The fact of the matter is that I had four children and a big yard with swings, slide, sandbox, and everything else. There were two children in nursery school whose fathers were ill and whose mothers had to work. It was impossible for the mothers to pick them up so I took them home with me. I gave them their dinner but asked that they play in the yard until I could get things ready. My children had to play outdoors too. At least when they come out in the open, you can deal with them.

Mrs. Walk: I know exactly where my difficulties are. I have felt, in the first place I'm the only young person in the building and the older teachers resent that I don't have their program and their discipline. I guess when I put the note up I was striking back. There's a great deal of resentment against me. Last year there was another young teacher in the building and they criticized her a lot. This year she's not here and I'm feeling all their resentment. It all boiled up and burst out with my note. This class is the only place where I find any acceptance at all from teachers.

Mr. Moustakas: Even when you know why people resent you, it still hurts very much.

Mrs. Walk: That's very true. It's very hard to shake it off. Yesterday I was called away from recess to straighten out a lumber bill. We needed it to build a stage. When I got back outside, I said to another teacher, "It's kind of cold out here, isn't it?" She retorted with sarcasm, "How would you know, you haven't been out here?"

Mrs. Cone: We have a teacher in our building with a sour disposition. Many times I come away with that feeling—in fact I'm cautious about expressing myself in front of her because I'm never sure.

Mrs. Allen: I don't go near people like that. I always keep my distance.

Mrs. Walk: I don't do that. I want her to understand me but I can feel so hurt talking to her. Why should I want to be near her? Why should I knock myself out when the situation is practically impossible? Anyway it's her life. It's up to her.

Mrs. Sall: Is it just this one person?

Mrs. Walk: No, everyone in the school.

Mrs. Hoch: I know how you feel. When I first taught in our building I felt the older teachers were always staring at me and what I did. Everytime I was in charge of a school function I got sick. I think it's why I never had any children of my own. I just put out all of my emotions trying to meet the other teachers' standards and never quite making the grade.

Mrs. Sall: I don't think we can size it up to young and old.

Mrs. Hoch: No, I never meant that.

Mr. Frank: You'd find the same thing wherever you worked. When I first started teaching I could have got into a great deal of trouble. I was given a sponsor. She thought her way of teaching was the only way. She brought one thing after another to me when I got ready to teach certain skills in arithmetic or reading. I could have said to her, "I'm sorry but we never learned to teach it that way in our methods classes at the university." But if I had talked that way to her, I would have spiked my guns with her right then and she would have made my life miserable. You'll find that in any job, I'm convinced. Wouldn't you say it takes a certain amount of tact?

Mrs. Walk: I know part of it is my fault. I've resented their surveillance and disapproval and I've bounced back at them.

Mrs. Dean: My school has been good. The older teachers have taught me a great deal but I have also observed some petty things, as you say.

Mrs. Long: The first day I appeared at my school on the recess I saw several teachers in a huddle. They got together to talk about me. One said, "I believe she's a Catholic." Another said, "Oh, no she seems all right to me, she couldn't be Catholic." If I had let that bother me—I said to myself, "Oh, well." She's retired now but I can definitely say she was my best friend in the school.

Mrs. Walk: That's the fine point. You said, "If I had let that bother me." If you're constructed so you don't become sensitive to things like that, you can talk to yourself and say, "Straighten up. Don't let these things bother you. Don't think about it. Don't feel it." But I can't do it.

Mrs. Long: Don't misunderstand me. Things bother me too. Mainly I was trying to show you, you are not alone in this problem.

Miss Whet: Do you feel you need their approval?

Mrs. Walk: No, I don't.

Miss Shawn: When I first came here to teach, I had a rugged time because all the other teachers had been at the school a long, long time. I was all alone. My supervisor never worked with anyone. It was hard for her to accept me there. I did things differently than she did.

She was at the North Pole and I was at the South Pole.
She had taken her training a long time ago and I was
just taking mine. I had different ideas and different
ways of doing things. Everything I did, according to her,
was all wrong. I could see what made her feel that way.
After a while, I understood it. I avoided issues with her,
kept my feelings inside. Once in a while I got awfully
tired of the great pretense. She even had me in tears
once. My children were always breaking the toys. My
children never put anything away. My children were
completely undisciplined. I kept saying to myself, "She
can't help it." I guess I could go on growing knowing
she was a sick person. I might be entirely wrong but it
helped me to understand why I threatened her and why
she resented anything I did that was new. I don't think
it's so much a question of your being younger. I think
they are teachers who stopped growing a long time ago
when they finished their training, and they resent your
broader insights. They criticize what you do, not because you are young but because your work involves
extra initiative and resourcefulness and understanding.

Comments

This meeting began in an exciting way. In the presence
of her principal, Mrs. Walk expresses her distress and disturbance in teaching, and describes her pretense at being a
strict teacher. She learns for the first time that her principal
supports her and approves of what she is doing in the classroom. Encouraged by his remarks, she ventures into another
problem in the school—the antagonistic and critical attitude
of other teachers when she attempts to face them in an open
fashion.

Her principal summarizes her problem in terms of a lack
of tact, but a number of teachers recognize her dilemma
and support her through experiences of their own. A few of

the teachers consider withdrawal from others the best solution, but most of them regard the open facing of conflicts as the best approach, even though the consequences might be painful and disturbing. There is a conviction in many of the teachers that the integrity of the teacher must be maintained, that this means calling upon sources of strength from within, and standing by one's values.

The self is not free to grow without this inner freedom of expression and development. Here for the first time Mrs. Walk, recognized and supported, is able to get a sense of her own being as a teacher and as a person. She can see her dishonest, false self in teaching, and begin to move toward an integration and consistency of self.

Fear and Freedom

Permitting children to be themselves, encouraging them to be open and spontaneous in their relations sometimes results in extreme behavior, in chaos and turmoil, especially in the beginning of such an experience and particularly with children who have not known the value and meaning of true freedom. It sometimes takes a long time for this phase of wild expression and hyperactivity to release the inhibitions and tensions of the past, to remove the externally imposed patterns and to discover the real self in worthwhile activity.

Teachers who want to provide for freedom of self expression often are afraid of the evaluations of other teachers and principals who regard noise and moving activities of children as signs of the teacher's breakdown and inability to control the group.

Expression of self may involve noise and activity but it also involves silence, inactivity, absorption and contemplation.

Freedom to be may mean simple satisfaction and joy in being itself. The experience of freedom of self does not have to lead to something else, does not have to be connected to the future or relate to growth or change. An expression of self can be significant as itself alone.

True acceptance of the learner contributes to the process of growth. The learner must feel he is loved as a person, experience his own development as significant, and know that he is valued both in his sheer being and in what he may become.

The excerpt below illustrates the fears connected with freedom and the tendency among teachers to look for change and activity as signs of growth rather than to value expressions of being.

Mrs. Dase: Young teachers are often afraid to act on their own spontaneous thoughts, to use their own judgment. That's what they need to learn to do. We've got some excellent young teachers in our school system. The old ones keep telling them how to teach, how to discipline, etc. They're not telling them the right way. If you young teachers would just go out and have the courage of your convictions, you'd do it the best way you know how and you'd be fine teachers. Don't be so worried about what old teachers think who are anxious to tell you how.

Miss Morse: Oh, it isn't that. They have more experience and can help us.

Mrs. Sall: They have the experience, I grant that, but they often lack sympathy and kindliness toward young teachers because they think they know so much about it. They don't give you young teachers a chance to work it out your own way. I've seen it happen again and again. If you follow their preaching, you'll turn out to be poor teachers because you can never really teach someone else's way.

Mr. Moustakas: Unless what you do comes from you, you cannot act on your own and have firm faith in yourself.

Mrs. Walk: I'll admit I was afraid to really try something new. All along I've been talking only on the surface. About a month ago I decided to give children the freedom of choice they want. Now I'm going through complete chaos and turmoil. I've been wondering whether the turmoil is really within me or in the class, whether it's all because I've got troubles. No one has even given me any techniques that really helped in a relationship. I'm very sensitive to the children's feelings during these times but I don't know what to do. A little girl came up to me a few days ago and said, "I hate you." She said it twice.

Miss Whet: Maybe she really does.

Mrs. Walk: Yes, but what can I do. Other children say things to each other. Other teachers have come into my room. They think I'm crazy to let it all go on. It doesn't bother me if that's the way the children really feel. Yes, it does bother me. I've been trying to figure out if it disturbs me because when I was in the second grade I had to maintain a stony silence. I remember I resented it but I have not been able to shake the need for a quiet room out of my system. All that's happening in my room is children are expressing themselves wildly. I'm not teaching reading, writing, and arithmetic.

Mrs. Sall: If the children are learning on their own, does it matter that you're not teaching?

Mrs. Walk: But there is noise all the time. When I try to get control of the room, I lose control of myself. They don't care about me. I go home at the end of the day and say, "I'm never going back. I'm going to quit teaching, give it up, retreat."

Mr. Moustakas: That kind of turmoil is extremely bad for you and the children. Is that it?

Mrs. Walk: Maybe I've given the wrong impression. I don't believe my room is what you'd call turmoil. But there are times when the children make plenty of noise and

I take ten minutes to quiet them. That's ten minutes wasted. Then they're all quiet. So what? Why should I feel I want to quit teaching?

Mr. Moustakas: The children in your group are bringing out strong feelings and this is troubling you.

Mrs. Walk: There is a funny thing about my situation as much as I hate it, as much as I dread going into the school room, at the same time for the first time in my life I feel secure at home. I feel more truly understood. I feel I am accepted, my qualifications and my limits.

Mr. Moustakas: You feel disturbed like the children in school but more satisfied with yourself at home.

Mrs. Walk: Perhaps the children feel that way too.

Mrs. Sall: The best thing to do in the classroom is to take the plunge and have the courage of your convictions. Give children the freedom to express themselves, regardless of school pressures. If it fails, drop it; if not, continue it no matter what. We keep on with workbooks and texts because they're quiet and safe activities.

Mrs. Allen: The problem of allowing that kind of freedom is too much noise.

Mrs. Sall: There are limits of course.

Miss Tars: What limits?

Mrs. Sall: Whichever we feel we must set. It will differ with each of us.

Mrs. Allen: What about the teachers around you, shouldn't they be considered?

Mrs. Sall: What are you suggesting, that I go around and ask the teachers next door and above and below me how much noise they can stand and keep just under the maximum?

Miss Shawn: I think the best way is to do what you feel is right and not ask your friends and neighbors.

Mrs. Dase: I think teachers are afraid to let children express themselves because they are afraid of what will happen.

Miss Whet (to Mr. Moustakas): You've said the classroom must convey freedom to the child so he can express his potentialities. I have told children during a free period they could do anything they'd like. You may tell the children they may draw. Some may draw the same thing everytime. Some just sit there silently.

Mrs. Sall: Every child is creative but he just can't get it out without the teacher's guidance. You have to give them an idea. Maybe I'm wrong, but I find that if I give them a general subject, they can draw anything in that area and can get up and talk about it.

Mr. Moustakas: I'm not so sure that a child's sitting silently is not his choice and of value. There is joy and satisfaction in sheer being. Not all significant experience has to be connected with growth. It can be significant and lead to nothing but itself. I remember sitting in silence with a child in play therapy for as long as five hours. If the child decides to remain silent and apparently inactive, absorbed in his own being, I accept this decision. Sometimes I think we're afraid that if we do not break the silence or interrupt inactivity, the child will remain static. We're more interested in change and becoming than we are in being.

Miss Whet: There's a pressure on us from parents to accomplish something with their children. If they were observing and saw their child just sitting silently, I fear they would be very critical of us.

Comments

In this meeting, Mrs. Walk searches for some key to her disturbance and confusion, to the difficulty which arises when she permits children to express themselves. She explores the ambivalent aspects of her feelings. She tells how her fear of trying something new in the classroom creates a conflict between *wanting* to give children more freedom and feeling that the classroom *should* be a quiet, orderly place. As she looks at the confusion in her classroom, she comes to an exciting discovery. With all the feeling of dread in facing the children, she finds a growing security at home and a feeling of being truly understood.

Mrs. Walk receives much support in the group as other teachers convey their own anxiety when children are free to express themselves. When the teacher permits freedom in the classroom, difficulties sometimes occur which constitute a real challenge and threat which the teacher must meet with courage, ingenious guidance, and an unyielding faith in the growth potentials of children.

In this session, some teachers show their concern over the quiet, inactive child and their need to get the child into concrete projects. The instructor attempts to show that being is worthwhile in itself. Sitting silently in absorption and thought or watching the beauties of a growing thing can be a significant educational experience.

Stealing

Sometimes teachers become critical of certain kinds of children's behavior, such as lying and stealing, and discover, in the process of exploring these acts and their own experience, comparable incidents in which they have been involved. In the excerpt below such a process of self-discovery occurs. There is strong disagreement and feeling in the group as to what constitutes an act of stealing.

Mr. Downs: In my class last year I had a wonderful boy in my room and I really liked him. He was absent and yesterday I learned he had stolen something from the dime store. I couldn't believe it. I was actually hurt to hear that he had stolen something. Today I saw him in the hall. I stopped him and said, "What's this I heard about you yesterday?" He sort of got all flushed and I said, "What happened?" and he said, "What do you

mean?" and I said, "What about the yo-yo?" He looked
at me. I said, "Was it true? At first I didn't believe it.
I was going to ask you." He said, "Yes." I said, "Why
did you do it? There must have been a reason." He said,
"I don't know." I really believed him. I said, "I think it
hurts you. And it hurts your teacher more than it hurts
you. I just can't believe it and neither can your teacher
believe it. You never will do a thing like that again, will
you?" He said, "No, I'll never do it again." I really felt
for that child. I don't think he'll do it again.

Mr. Moustakas: It is upsetting to find out that somebody—

Mr. Downs: Yes, somebody I would trust with anything.

Mrs. Sall: I think practically all of my friends went through
a stage of snitching anything they could get out of a
dime store until they put glass tops on. They were just
taking things all the time. I think it was just for the joy
of doing it. None of them turned out to be criminals.
I'm not saying that I think it is right but I can remember
it very clearly.

Mrs. Cone: Dime store stealing. I know of several girls who
did it in the seventh and eighth grade. They had been
stealing for a long, long time. I often thought if I should
have said or done anything about it. I never did. They
are perfectly lovely juniors and seniors at the high school
this year. I don't think it would dawn on them to steal
now. It was certainly something. They would count the
loot to see who could get the most. It wasn't a question
of money at all or lack of things to do or family interest.
I often wondered why they enjoyed it.

Mrs. Sall: Something people go through. They get the excitement out of it then they forget it, and that's that.

Mrs. Dase: I don't think you realize you are pinching instead of stealing.

Miss Whet: Is it an adventure or what?

Mr. Downs: People say they're pinching it or they're taking
it but that's no different from stealing. They take things

and say it is just a prank. They call it a prank or something else, but it's still stealing. They don't know if they won't accept the act for what it really is or what. That's what I can't understand. It really is a wrong thing to do.

Miss Morse: Like towels and ash trays, I've done it on vacation, taken quite a few ash trays.

Mrs. Sall: That's the same with children taking things—

Miss Morse: It's more of a souvenir.

Mr. Downs: But you are supposed to buy them. You are stealing.

Mrs. Sall: It's a feeling of independence, taking something and getting away with it. It's something of a thrill.

Mr. Downs: I like people who don't steal, when they say "No, I should not take those things." There's an honest, dependable person.

Mrs. Sall: It's not stealing. It's just a souvenir.

Mrs. Allen: That's rationalizing. Aren't you stealing when you take something that doesn't belong to you?

Mr. Frank: You talk about stealing things. Isn't it just as bad to steal time, getting off work for half an hour when no one is looking?

Mr. James: I've seen that. Some men building a house were supposed to have a half hour for lunch. They still hadn't returned after 45 minutes. One said, "Well, we've had our hands in Johnson's pocket for 15 minutes now."

Mr. Frank: I think if we would go over this whole class, person by person, and if they would tell the honest truth, most of us have been guilty of stealing at some time or other. If you look back, now I look back at the time when I've stolen watermelons. There's a certain thrill of taking. I don't know just how you would explain it but there is a thrill there. I think oftentimes, children want to experience that thrill of doing something that society or their parents or somebody has told them not to do.

Comments

Mr. Downs begins this discussion with the expression of his strong feeling that stealing is wrong. He gets some support from Mrs. Allen.

Mrs. Sall disagrees and puts stealing on a relative basis, considers it part of a developmental stage that people go through. Mrs. Cone states that many of the children who stole in the junior grades are among the best citizens in high school. Some members of the group note that, in a certain sense, everyone steals, if not tangible items, then time and other intangibles.

The session does not show any basic change in the initial attitudes and concepts of the people who expressed themselves but possibly it led to a more tolerant understanding of the child who steals.

Self-Acceptance, Sorrow, and Guilt

Teachers are vitally concerned with the consequences of their own behavior. They want to act fairly and honestly in situations. Sometimes they feel unsure of themselves. They do not know what is right. They search for an interpretation of self-acceptance that will have validity in the complex realities of mass education. When they act wrongly or are inconsistent with human values, when they do harm or commit cruel acts, they feel sorry, troubled, and guilty. They want to enhance the self and when they hurt and destroy rather than create healthy situations, they suffer inwardly. This struggle to understand self-acceptance, sorrow, and guilt is illustrated in the excerpt below.

Mrs. Sall: I've been thinking about the self-accepting person. Wouldn't he be an unbearable egotist?

Mr. Moustakas: You think he's completely self-sufficient and self-satisfied.

Mrs. Long: I don't think anyone is completely self-accepting.

Miss Whet: I think such a person could be extremely disturbed.

Mrs. Dase: I think one can be completely self-accepting as a person without being completely self-satisfied.

Miss Shawn: I don't think it's a person who is overbearing. He accepts everything, including criticism.

Mrs. Sall: I believe this person would modify his behavior to avoid hurting others.

Mrs. Wull: The self-accepting person leaves others alone to be themselves. He's not dominated nor does he dominate. These are people you can trust open-heartedly.

Mrs. Sall: Is self-acceptance something to strive for like, for instance, "goodness," that you probably never reach completely.

Mrs. Long: I would say self-acceptance is a goal everyone should strive to reach but not worry if it is not fully achieved.

Mrs. Dase: I think it is just an experience, a part of living.

Mrs. Wull: When a child realizes your acceptance, all problems in the relation are solved. When they sense we share with them a feeling of loyalty, sincerity, and love, all conflicts and battles are over. They don't get it from us, unless we feel it inside. They sense acceptance from us and feel it as individuals in the group.

Mr. Frank: I would like to report progress. I would have spanked a child last week had I not been a member of this group. I almost did but not quite. I remembered our discussion on acceptance and did not spank.

Miss Whet: I had the same experience. Something about this class made me stop and think, but I can't say what it was. I think I would have felt guilty had I spanked the child.

Mr. Downs: Do you think that guilt comes when you do all you feel you should?

Mr. Wann: I think your conscience is clear if you feel that you've done everything you could have done.

Mrs. Wull: Is guilt an indication of lack of self-acceptance? Can a person feel guilty and at the same time self-accepting?

Mr. Wann: I suppose it depends upon the individual.

Miss Tars: We see all the things the child is lacking, and we want him to catch up and the first thing you know we become frustrated.

Miss Shawn: Yes, I know I'm guilty of that too. We expect too much to happen in a short time.

Miss Tars: I think we get very frustrated when we know there are certain children that we should know better in order to help them; but when you've got all these pressures from parents and administrators, you're busy every minute of the day. Why you feel terrible when you think of all the children you have failed to reach. I wonder why we just don't all crack up.

Mrs. Sall: And sometimes you're in a hurry and you say something that you know wasn't right to say to a child and the situation is gone. Very few people seem to realize that teachers worry deeply.

Miss Tars: I know sometimes I go home and people say, "Go and hide somewhere or something."

Miss Morse: Maybe teachers should learn to let things bounce off.

Mrs. Sall: You can't ignore your behavior when you feel you've done something wrong.

Mrs. Cone: May I say something here. A couple of years ago I had two little girls that came up to my room from Mexico, I believe. They were quite dark-skinned. When they came in, the teachers in the building looked at them. They were not just like the rest of the children in the school. I was very much concerned because I wanted these children to be happy. In a few days a teacher noticed lice in their hair. She immediately spread the news through the building. Immediately everybody looked at them. To make it worse, the safety girls, the patrol girls, the service squad girls knew it. "Lice girls," that's what they called them. I go along with what you say. I feel when we do that to children—any child—we have to account for it and pay with a sick conscience.

Mr. Downs: I feel that's right. If you've really hurt someone, your feeling of guilt is more painful than the damage you caused the other person. You're the one who suffers and you cannot accept yourself. That's a terrible feeling.

Miss Tars: There is a difference between feeling sorry and feeling guilty.

Mr. Wann: That's what I would think. You feel sorry when you make a mistake but you feel guilty when you consciously make a wrong choice. Do you see what I mean? Mistakes are made unwillingly.

Mr. Moustakas: The guilty feeling is much deeper, more pervasive and it lasts.

Mr. Wann: It's all right just to think, "I'm sorry," but the other is worse, it's inside.

Miss Tars: I can feel sorry about something, about an honest mistake, but not feel guilty and when I say I'm sorry, I really am sorry.

Mrs. Hoch: Suppose that what you did was in the best interest of what you thought was right and it turned out to be wrong. Then it would be a kind of feeling sorry.

Mr. Frank: I feel guilty within myself when I willfully make wrong choices.

Miss Shawn: Maybe feeling guilty is a matter of degree. You might on the whole accept yourself and yet may feel guilty occasionally for acting out of character.

Mr. Frank: I would think it would have to be.

Mr. Wann: I think in the death of someone very close, I have found that feeling of guilt is greater in my heart and within myself because it is absolutely irrevocable and I can't do anything for that person. It suddenly brings out some things I had done or might have done while that person was alive. I have known two or three times that feeling of guilt and it is so terrific.

Mrs. Wull: I believe that time heals, the feeling of guilt lessens through time alone.

Mrs. Dase: Wouldn't it depend on how much you dwell over it, think about it, reflect back to it, or whether you put it out of your mind?

Mrs. Sall: I've taught school as long as most of the people in this room. And starting way back to my beginning seeing how children were manhandled. I punished children physically too, though not in recent years. I don't believe there is a single time that I haven't felt guilty afterwards.

Mr. Moustakas: Always felt disturbed after spanking a child.

Mrs. Sall: Yes! There has been a feeling of guilt within me and I have wanted to do something good to make up for it.

Mr. Frank: If we can't change our attitudes and behavior, wouldn't we be in school in vain?

Mrs. Wull: As we go on with experience, we hope we can rise above the apparent limitations of a situation. When we can't get over things with our minds we can do things with our hands. We can talk about our guilt with our children. They can help us loosen up as we help them. Then our relations are more honest and more loving.

Comments

The self-accepting person is seen in different ways in the group. Some believe this person to be an egotist, extremely disturbed, and self-satisfied. Others see him as loyal, trustworthy, and open-hearted, as a person who leaves others to be themselves, does not hurt or dominate, and is not dominated by others. Finally self-acceptance is seen as an experience, an expression of life.

Two teachers state they sometimes do not want to spank a child but feel they should. This leads to a discussion of guilt and how it influences the teacher's behavior. The intrinsic nature of conscience is raised here—the feeling of an inward knowing that an act against another is morally wrong. One's sense of conscience creates the guilt resulting from a conscious, deliberate wrong choice. As the discussion continues, there is an interesting differentiation made between guilt and sorrow and how these feelings operate in concrete situations. This discussion is an example of how teachers work together to learn more fully the detailed nature of their own feelings, not as abstractions or reflections but as aspects of their own personal experiences. Mrs. Wull offers an unusual solution: "We can talk about our guilt with our children. They can help us loosen up as we help them. Then our relations are more honest and more loving."

Conclusion

Only in his whole being, in all his spontaneity, can the teacher come to realize his possibilities. Expression of experience is a process in which insights develop and in which the learner is growing and attaining appreciation of his sense of self. We must encourage these self-perceptions and explorations of the individual and convey our respect for his personal discoveries. Then the learner is free to realize that his own organism is trustworthy, that it is a suitable instrument for discovering satisfying behavior in each situation (6). When free from pressures, the teacher knows himself, relates this self-knowledge to others, and grows in the very act of expression.

Diagnosis and analysis, though not destructive approaches in themselves, often lead the individual to substitute partial, non-experimental language, and fragmented truths, for the unity of thought and feeling, the wholeness of experience. There is also a tendency in analysis and evaluation to look for appearances, common categories and explanations, to make the personal impersonal rather than to search for the personal reality of an experience. There is the danger that values and convictions will become nothing at all. It is critically important for the development of positive freedom that personal spontaneity be encouraged.

The process of growth is an individual, personal one and occurs in significant, vital experience and self-exploration. The individual must be himself, free to express what he wants. The individual must discover the values, meanings, insights, and errors in life's experiences for unless *he* discovers them for himself, they remain undiscovered and have no relationship to the self. The process begins with real self-expression in unified consistent behavior, and eventuates in the development of a unique and responsible personality.

Given a choice, the teacher acts in accordance with his real self. He selects certain values inherent to his unique experience and to what is universally good for man. He naturally is cooperative when he is free to be himself. This cooperative attitude carries conviction. It leads to healthy relationships, relationships which cannot be ruled, ordered, or demanded by authority but which will emerge in an atmosphere which recognizes, respects and nurtures the tendency of organisms toward self-actualization.

References

1. Commission on Teacher Education. *Teachers For Our Times.* Washington, D. C.: American Council on Education, 1944.
2. Dewey, John. *Democracy and Education.* New York: The Macmillan Co., 1916.
3. James, William. *Talks to Teachers on Psychology: And*

to Students on Some of Life's Ideals. New York: Henry Holt & Co., 1919.

4. May, Rollo. *Man's Search for Himself.* New York: W. W. Norton & Company, Inc., 1953.

5. Rasey, Marie. *It Takes Time.* New York: Harper & Brothers, 1953.

6. Rogers, Carl R. What It Means to Become a Person in *The Self.* Ed. by Clark E. Moustakas, New York: Harper & Brothers, 1956.

THE TEACHER'S EXPRESSION OF SELF
IN RELATIONS WITH CHILDREN

As teachers, we must realize that all true and lasting education is self-education, a process which begins only when the individual proposes to learn. We often can make learning possible for another by providing information, the setting, initiating an atmosphere, offering materials and other resources, and by being present in the full human sense, listening, empathizing, supporting, and encouraging. We can strive as teachers to foster conditions that widen the horizon of others and give them command of their powers, so that they can find their own happiness in their own way (2).

In the true learning situation, the teacher must be an open person. When he is open to his own experiences as a learner, the teacher becomes fully alive. In openness there is a willingness to let experiences accumulate and sink in and ripen. This is essential to one's own becoming. Rasey and Menge (3, p. 39) state the matter clearly in a creative account of the educative process: "The learner can come to his nurturers, but the transaction is achieved only when the nurturer can open himself to the learner and the learner can open to him."

The educational situation which most effectively promotes learning is one in which (a) the uniqueness of the learner is deeply respected and treasured and (b) the person is free to explore the relationships, ideas, materials, and resources available to him in the light of his own particular interests, potentialities, and experience. We need through education to seek to develop citizens who are free to respond to their own emotions, accept the guidance of their own thinking, and pursue their own ends. This does not mean that original feelings, thoughts, and purposes are always sound but through continuous experience of self-expression and self-criticism, purpose and emotion, as well as thought, may become disciplined and refined (1).

The teacher's relationships with children contain many different values, interests, and concerns. The nature of these relationships tells whether the teacher is an alive and growing person in the classroom or frightened, static, and unfree. Given an opportunity teachers want to explore their relations with children, not in a report or as cases for analysis, but rather, as processes in which the teacher expresses his experience with all the personal involvement and relevance. In the act of expression, the teacher often discovers new meanings, positive approaches to the child and the resolution of existing problems. A number of classroom relations have been selected to illustrate the nature and process of self-exploration and its meaning and value for the individual teacher.

The Child Rejected by Other Children

Mrs. Sall: I'm trying to figure out the best way to refer a child for special services.

Mrs. Long: You should talk this over with your principal.

Mrs. Dase: I feel you should discuss it first with the mother. Could you?

Mrs. Sall: Yes, I think she can be approached as a wonderful mother. She is sensitive. I think I've been reluctant to tell her something is wrong. If she wasn't such a grand person I could dislike her for what she's done to the child. But she is so wonderful I don't want to add to her burdens. I really don't think I'm the one to talk with her.

Mr. Moustakas: You're afraid if you told her it would be very disturbing to her.

Mrs. Sall: That's right. I don't know what she would do. She's our room mother and she's done so much. I know I shouldn't let that enter in. The child should come first but I just don't want to add to her troubles. I don't know what he lacks but he hasn't done any school work in two months. I get after him and he cries or he crawls under the table or hates school and doesn't want to come back. He'll hate you one minute and love you the next. In spite of it all he's a lovely little reader, and does his workbook without any instruction. I didn't think he'd ever be able to read. I don't know when he concentrates. He never seems to be looking when I'm instructing. But he's so entirely babyish. I've seen little two-year olds act like that. His mother was quite surprised when I told her he could read and that he does work difficult for my top group.

Miss Tars: The child accepted in the group?

Mrs. Sall: The child isn't very well accepted by the group. His mother is very clever at making puppets and she puts on puppet shows and the children who were invited to the party were just wonderful to Bill until the party, and then after that they dropped him again. It was so obvious. They were so tickled they were invited to the puppet show and after the party was over, he was the same child picked on again. I can't get him to converse. The only thing I get is "so and so hit me." Of course he started it. I've seen it over and over again. For no reason at all he hits. The mother tried to have him take the bus at noon because the children were cruel to him in the riding group. He is very awkward, quite large, but there must be something there or he couldn't read like he does.

Mrs. Dase: Do you mean the mother would be in the car and ignore all this that goes on?

Mrs. Sall: Well, she doesn't ignore him in her heart but she tries not to say too much to the children because she says she really doesn't understand how much of it is Bill's fault. I can see her position too.

Mrs. Dase: I don't know why the parents would just sit and not try to do something about that in some way.

Mrs. Sall: I build Bill up. I try to do it constantly by remembering how well he reads. I build him up in everything he does but what he doesn't do is so obvious. He's such a pest with other children. It's hard to build him up and have the children respect him one minute and not the next. Sometimes he gets wild with his hitting. He goes through all kinds of facial gestures. When the mother comes, she takes over the whole thing. She does everything well.

Miss Whet: I think it's a shame when parents give parties for children and then show off their own cleverness.

Mrs. Sall: Well, but the children were really interested in the puppet show. He's a child who will share his crayons, paper, pencils. I think he does it mainly with a will-you-be-my-friend attitude.

Miss Whet: He's buying friendship.

Mrs. Sall: He feels he must pay for everything he gets. He acts cantankerous when he's rejected by the other children.

Mr. Moustakas: Then he hurts others because he expects them to turn against him.

Mrs. Sall: There's a neighborhood feeling against him too. The poor child is just crucified it seems to me. For what? I don't know except he hits. I've had note after note from parents saying, "Please don't let my child sit next to Billy." What am I going to do? Of course, I've never told the mother. She hears it all the time in the riding group and in the neighborhood. As I say I just lack the courage to tell the mother.

Mr. Frank: I would be interested in knowing if the neighbors think she's such a splendid person. That's the big question in my mind.

Mrs. Walk: I would also like to know how the family stands in the neighborhood, what the other mothers and fathers say about the family.

Mrs. Sall: That would be a hard thing for me to do.

Mr. Frank: Sometimes you get it voluntarily without asking.

Mrs. Sall: But she's so wonderful. If I find a little boy crying and say, "I'm going to take him home," she'll say, "Don't bother, I'll take him home."

Mrs. Walk: Would a child accept a ride with her?

Mrs. Sall: Oh yes! They think she's very nice and talk kindly to her.

Mrs. Cone: I had a similar situation. I had a mother last year who had an only child and this little girl was just as backward as a child could be and her mother was constantly getting her into Brownies and other groups. She was a member of the PTA, very active in the room, came about twice a week to see what was going on. As far as the little girl was concerned I think it was all wasted. I think she thought she was doing all that for the child. The child wasn't interested at all. It just made her go back into her shell because her mother was the active type and the girl was more passive. She wouldn't come forth with anything which her mother did. She put her in ballet school and brought things to school for her to show and the little girl didn't appreciate any of it. The other children didn't care for the girl because of her personality. I do think with older parents many expect too much of them, but I think it's just the opposite here. I think they've done everything for this child and it's all been wasted because the child never learned to do anything for herself.

Mrs. Sall: But this little Bill, he comes up and kisses me and anyone else he feels like. He's rather an affectionate little youngster and Tom who is a very sophisticated youngster said, "Bill has to kiss the teacher all the time. He's a baby." Bill looked at me and said, "I don't have to kiss you all the time, do I? I would kill you if I wanted to, but I won't. I love you."

Mrs. Walk: Is his mother just facing the situation now?

Mrs. Sall: No! She had many conferences with the kindergarten teacher last year. They talked it all over and the teacher suggested Bill be retained. The doctor suggested this too. So did the principal. The mother agreed but the first day of school she brought him to my room against everybody's advice.

Miss Shawn: It seems to me she was more worried about what the neighbors would think than about the child's welfare. But you say he's a good reader and does his work well.

Mrs. Sall: Yes, but he hasn't written a single word since he's been here.

Miss Shawn: But he is a good reader.

Mrs. Sall: Yes, but I don't understand how. I introduce a word once and it's his forever and he doesn't seem to be listening.

Mrs. Wull: He'll catch on to writing one of these days. I had a child who didn't write all year in first grade but he writes beautifully now.

Mrs. Long: Maybe he's really very bright. Do you think he would have benefited by remaining in kindergarten?

Mrs. Sall: I don't believe so. I don't know what holding him back would have done to him.

Mr. Wann: Maybe he's just an individual chap who isn't going to be molded or pushed around. I always hated

writing and still don't do it except when I'm forced to.
I think I'd worry more about his personal happiness
than about academic work. I have a feeling that when
he proposes to learn himself that he'll do it.

Mrs. Sall: Are you advising me not to even speak to him
about his work?

Mr. Wann: I'm not offering advice, just giving my reaction.

Miss Whet: If I were you I'd put the whole thing up to his
mother. It doesn't work to force him to do school work.
There's no point continuing it. Try to get the parents to
help.

Mrs. Sall: What about when he's disturbing others?

Mrs. Dase: Could you let him do something constructive he
wants to do? Could you get some books for him to read?

Miss Whet: It sounds as though his parents have never let
him do things on his own.

Mrs. Allen. These older parents often go along with a child
and do his thinking for him and don't give the child a
chance to learn to take care of himself.

Mrs. Long: Is there anyone in the room he likes real well?

Mrs. Sall: He tries to like them all. He'll go up to one and
say something nice and they'll shove him away and I'm
very sympathetic and that makes me always feel—I always try to build him up. In fact I sent him off to the
kindergarten the other day with a book to read to his
former teacher and while he was gone I told them not
to make remarks. I told about some children that had
their teeth and some that did not and some that hadn't
lost any yet, just to show them that children will grow
differently and that his hand could not maybe write just
now like the others. Just like second teeth, some have
lost their first teeth and some haven't. I said, "Just see
the difference how we grow. Now Bill just can't do it."
I didn't know how to explain it to them because they
were just making such fun of him for a long time.
They've never made fun of his work since then. I feel

somehow I can't bring out what the child has. I feel an inadequacy there, whether I can't inspire him or what I don't know. I've taught a good many years and I've never had a child like this.

Mr. Moustakas: You would like him to write?

Mrs. Sall: I would like to know what I could do to make him want to write.

Mrs. Wull: Do you remember Jimmy, that child that wouldn't write? The thing I'm thinking of particularly was there was quite a lot of upsetness in the room and he was given a large clump of paper and a new pencil and told he could just scribble all he wanted. Do you remember? And he started in and all he would do is just make these great big circles. In three weeks' time, I think we decided that if he did anything that looked like a letter that I would point it out, "well, this is a nice 'O,'" and he made two or three O's and I think "A" was the next letter that he did. And it went on, but he certainly had a lot of that to get out of his system and it was treated respectfully. Out of this very large movement he began making just two or three letters. Of course he did have other physiological situations there, but he developed so much. He could go to the board or do it on paper. He seemed to have a drive all the time to do something and he didn't know what he wanted to do. And finally after a month, he was writing words.

Mrs. Sall: Maybe I could try that (pause) and just ignore the very fact that he doesn't finish his work.

Mrs. Whet: Are you going to talk with his mother?

Mrs. Sall: I don't think so. I just thought that maybe if she could feel he was getting along, there would be a different feeling in the air. Then they'd think more of him.

Miss Dean: I think there's an awful lot to his being an only child. It's awfully hard when you have to make that break from your parents. I know it was for me. I wouldn't have gotten on a bus for anything without my mother. I wanted them in a big crowd. I wanted to be shown. And it stayed with me even though I was mature in other ways. I was all right after I went through it once. But it was such an awful feeling—doing something for the first time on your own, until really I was pretty big. And it was kind of a blow when I finally had to. I've overcome it now, but gee, I think I was at college. I'm ashamed to say it but I was a big girl and afraid even to buy my own clothes for fear I'd make a mistake. My mother never pushed me. She just kept doing things for me.

Mr. Moustakas: It's easy to see why you would be so frightened about going somewhere or doing something on your own, some new experience.

Mr. Frank: But she turned out all right. It seems that we overcome a lot of things that happen when we are children.

Comments

Mrs. Sall starts this discussion apparently interested only in information. After her initial comments, she feels free to venture into the special problem she faces in the classroom and, specifically, in relation to one of the mothers. It seems clear that Mrs. Sall is not just reporting but is actually exploring the nature of her own personal feelings and experience. As she talks, some of her questions, confusions, and doubts begin to disappear. She sees new possibilities in her relationship with Bill and Bill's mother. Some of the teachers in the group are concerned mainly with the background of the child and the conditions impinging on the child. Others encourage her to maintain her faith in the child's potentialities. Mr. Wann refers to the uniqueness of the child and suggests that the child will learn when he himself proposes to learn and not from external direction. Mrs. Sall listens and learns. She emerges with her own conclusion not to talk with the mother, believing that the mother must continue to feel that school is one place where her child is doing well, and hoping that in time this will lead to a "different feeling in the air" at home.

Mrs. Sall's decision not to destroy the mother's illusion will undoubtedly be questioned. When she began to relate her reluctance to approach the mother the group on the whole felt she was not facing up to the issue, but as she continued to explore the problem, most of the group became convinced that Mrs. Sall's decision to maintain a wholly positive relation with the mother, to let the mother continue to feel that her son was making progress in school, and to continue to work toward a happier school life for the child was a meaningful, logical, and healthy solution.

The Child Rejected by the Teacher

Miss Shawn: To me it's very funny that some people think only of how to take care of their child when he is naughty, when he gets out of order. There must be something more to living with children than that.

Miss Tars: I think we focus on the problems because they seem all-important in our relations. I have a boy in my group, everytime I think of him I think, "How am I going to manage him." It all comes to one point. I don't accept him. I haven't from the very first day he walked into my door. He does everything he should not do and gets under my skin. Twice today I sent him out of the group. He irritates me so. As long as I feel this way, I know I won't get anywhere with him.

Mr. Frank: Aren't you afraid that he won't meet your requirements?

Miss Tars: Yes. (Pause.) Socially he isn't developing. Maybe I'm expecting too much but he is quite a case. I feel that maybe someone else could do better with him.

Miss Whet: I know what you mean. I have a child who is quite annoying. He's capable of doing his work but he keeps putting it off. This morning he got mad at somebody so he said he wasn't going outdoors. I said, "Why aren't you going outside?" "I'm mad." "Why are you mad?" I asked him. "I'm just mad." He does everything in reverse. I try to expect of him what I expect of all children but I feel I always compromise.

Mr. Moustakas: You are inconsistent with him then?

Miss Whet: I do with him what I wouldn't do with other children. I don't know what to do about it. I don't know how to explain him to the group. When he wants to borrow something no one will lend it because he's so ornery. They don't want to help him.

Mrs. Wull: When he's out of the room sometime, you could say to the children, "As long as we're on this earth there will always be people who need special help and understanding. He needs a bit more help from you and from me."

Mrs. Dase: I think in time children will accept him. I have one like that and children take it for granted that this child acts differently.

Mrs. Sall: It does help to explain it to them. They become very eager to help. They seem to like the child better after the explanation. It gives them something to do. I've seen it work a number of times. They even stop hitting back. Finally the child learns not to want to hit any more. You tell them it's nice when they help. They'll feel better inside.

Mrs. Long: But, if you explain, you have to be extremely careful it doesn't come back to the child or you may get a terrific explosion.

Mrs. Sall: That's true.

Miss Dean: Well, I have a child. He needs a great deal of help. This child got along pretty well without any mishaps until today. I debated seriously about putting a grade on the child's paper because I knew it would make him unhappy. But in relation to the other children's work, that's what he had. I started to leave it off but I decided that I wouldn't. I talked to him about it. I told him that sometimes we learn by seeing our errors and correcting them. But still it wasn't too long before the child became ill and very unhappy. (Pause). And the next thing I knew his head was down and he had become ill and vomited. I don't want him to become unacceptable to the children because he needs them and he has been getting a good response. We sent for someone to come and clean it up. When the children came back in the afternoon, they asked me what had happened to Don. I said, "Well, we all feel bad sometimes. He just felt bad. He was sick." They said, "He did that all last year." I added, "Sometimes we have a headache. It's just sort of like that. When he feels bad, that's what it makes him do." I don't know whether I'm going to know just the right road to travel with this child, to give him what he needs.

Mr. Moustakas: Getting the low grade was a very disturbing experience for him?

Miss Dean: Yes. That's the first time I've done it. Now that I see the trouble it brought I think I'll not grade his work any more.

Mrs. Allen: Wouldn't it be wise to speak to the children about it?

Miss Dean: That approach might be all right for some teachers but not for me.

Mr. Wann: Sometimes when there's a personality clash between a teacher and a child it's best to transfer the child to another room. I have seen it work out that way where another teacher can take the individuality of the child and work along with him. I have transferred children like that when it was necessary, with some pretty nice results. I've had teachers bring a child to the office and they were just shaking with rage. They were ready to disintegrate before they could say a word.

Miss Whet: I don't think it's fair to the other teacher. She may not be able to accept the child either.

Mrs. Dase: I think it a very bad thing to take a child out of your room just because you can't get along with him.

Miss Dean: I feel the child would really have to want to go to the other room before he could be happy.

Mr. Wann: That would be my job to sell him the idea of the other room.

Miss Morse: If the child is battling with the teacher he often doesn't want to move because that is an acknowledgment of his own failure. Often the child dislikes the teacher and the teacher will say, "I just can't like this child. I can't do anything with him." The child would know that, so that when the administration wanted to move the child to another room, he wouldn't want to go. He wants to stay where he is. To move is to accept a further rejection of him by the teacher.

Mrs. Sall: I wouldn't like a child taken from me that way. It would make me feel I was incapable of dealing with the situation. Wouldn't it be better to work harder to try to accept the child?

Mr. Wann: But there are some teachers who would not try to accept the child as you would try to do. Then, it would be a bad situation, wouldn't it?

Mrs. Wull: I don't think a teacher ever really dislikes a child. Something inside won't let her.

Miss Morse: I've had that feeling, just repulsed by the child and thought "What am I going to do? I don't want people to know I'm failing with the child." I had six awful weeks but I just had to like that child and make him like me.

Mrs. Allen: What if it doesn't work?

Mrs. Wull: I think when you want to care, it works every
time.

Comments

The child who constantly irritates the teacher is a difficult person to live with. In this session, Miss Tars recognizes that she cannot create opportunities for a child's
growth as long as she rejects him. She can only push him
into new activities, force him to meet her requirements, and
make him increasingly angry. The anger and resentment of
the child is expressed in all he does, and is stamped irrev-
ocably in his work.

Miss Whet relates a similar experience and recognizes
that her treatment of the child is unfair, compromising, and
vacillating.

Miss Dean explores her anxiety with a child who becomes ill whenever she pressures or evaluates him. She sees
the harm in knowingly forcing the child into a situation
that frightens and disturbs him. She seems to become aware,
in the course of the discussion, that when the child is sick
and angry, his feelings flow into his work and affect everything he does. When the work contains enraged expressions
of self rather than positive expression of the real self, there
is no continuity or growth.

Mr. Wann believes the problem can be solved by transferring the child to another room, but Miss Dean feels
that unless the child really wants to leave, a transfer forces
him to experience an increased feeling of rejection and
greater anxiety in self-expression. Miss Morse stresses the
value of self-determination in such relations in her comment: "I had six awful weeks but I just had to like that
child and make him like me." She gives the group something for further contemplation: *rejection in a relation is*

never resolved by transferring the child to another room.
The transfer is an ultimate kind of rejection that dissipates
any hope of a new and healthy relation between teacher and
child. Painful as it may be the change must occur in the
relationship or the growth potential is denied.

The Delinquent Child

Miss Whet: We have in our building a boy who is quite a
problem with other children. He's well on his way to
being a delinquent. He demands money from them or
threatens to beat them up. The other children have been
instructed to stay away from him and the teachers are
almost as afraid of him as the children. He is terrible
in class and definitely a mental problem. Today he
picked on a girl. Shoved her right out into the street
as far as he could and knocked her down. He had a wild
grin on his face. He was really pleased. He tried to
string a boy up in the lavatory about three weeks ago,
tried to hang him, but a teacher came in in time. It's
really frightening. The children come to the teacher for
a solution and she has none to offer. Everybody knows
if somebody doesn't help him he's going to become one
of the ten most wanted criminals in the country. Everybody in the building just looks at him and shakes their
head. He does odd things to get attention, queer actions
like getting a Mohawk haircut. Someone should be able
to help him. You wonder how many terrible things he'll
do. (Pause). You feel as if you could have done something to help him.

Mrs. Allen: Maybe he's beyond our help. Maybe we'd do
him a service to send him to another school.

Mrs. Long: Maybe that's so but if we had helped him
sooner, would he be so bad?

Miss Whet: Well this youngster is bad for a very good reason. Some children are good for very bad reasons and

some are bad for good reasons. This started years ago.

Miss Shawn: It's easy to think of reasons why he's that way but that doesn't help him any.

Mrs. Wull: I think taking him out of school and moving him around just encourages misbehavior.

Mr. Frank: I want to say one thing here. A few years ago I wrote a story of the worst child in our building, the most hopeless charge. I predicted in my own mind that he would become a criminal. I thought he was already delinquent. I wrote up his history from the time he entered school. I kept it in my confidential file. This boy did not turn out as I predicted at all, for which I am very happy. Today he's a pretty fair citizen. Think of the damage I may have done him if I had publicly labeled him a potential criminal. After that, I destroyed my confidential files.

Mrs. Dase: I remember this boy. We created a special atmosphere of freedom and trust for him. Sometimes we didn't seem to be making any progress at all.

Mr. Frank: Believe me you did. Certainly something must have changed.

Mrs. Dase: But I don't know what we did.

Mr. Frank: Somehow you must have created an atmosphere where he could accept himself.

Mrs. Long: I don't think there's any sure way of predicting anything, but if you feel, when you see a child in this predicament that something should be done, the sooner the better. The way it is now, this other boy is pre-delinquent. Practically everyone in school knows who he is. And he's just a lone wolf, and if he stays in this situation he will get worse and worse. I don't feel that this is the place for him. The relationship he has formed with the social worker is absolutely remarkable. Because he was playing on the Junior League baseball team, he made an appointment to be in her office at 7:00 in the morning. He thinks that much of her, and is able to tell the things to her that have happened, and his feelings about them. Even if he had to walk down there, he wouldn't miss it. There's a person who really understands him and likes him. And I think this worker realizes, too, that he is just the one person in his world. He has a very wonderful relationship. But he is so antagonistic in school and so against the world for hating him, all the way along the line. He has gone into this relationship quite intensively for the last six months. And of course, he is going to get worse before he gets better. I just wanted to add that people in school can't get next to him because he feels that he is hated all the way around, because he has no friends.

Mr. Downs (to Mr. Moustakas): Do you think we should accept this child?

Mr. Moustakas: I think you can have standards and values which differ from this child but still accept him.

Mrs. Sall: How can you accept him when you have that inward feeling "Oh I wish he wouldn't say that or do that." I don't accept him, I don't do anything about it.

Mr. Moustakas: Perhaps you simply cannot accept him.

Mrs. Sall: But I don't want to feel that way.

Mr. Moustakas: You feel it without being able to help yourself.

Mrs. Sall: That's it exactly.

Miss Dean: She's as bad as the child, in spite of her wishes.

Miss Whet: Maybe his worker can accept him because she isn't so close to the situation. She cannot see the harm and suffering he brings to others.

Mr. Moustakas: You mean that it's easier to accept a child when you are not involved in his everyday life?

Mrs. Sall: Yes, that's true. I can see that the other is a more vital kind of acceptance.

Comments

In this discussion Miss Whet begins with a strong feeling that a child in her school is well along the way to delinquency. She starts by seeing only the terrifying implications of living with an extremely hostile child and ends with a feeling that school people in the child's life could help him.

Mrs. Allen states that there is no possible help in school for the delinquent child. Other teachers enter the discussion pointing out that through acceptance and love even the child classified as a delinquent responds. Mr. Frank relates past experience to show the danger of labeling a child as a delinquent. He points to his own pessimism and exclaims that in an atmosphere of freedom and trust even the most "hopeless charge" can make important personality changes and become a responsible citizen. Something happens, but how and what? Mrs. Dase states, "We didn't seem to be making any progress at all" and "But I don't know what we did." Perhaps it was the initiation of an atmosphere of freedom and trust which enabled the child to discover positive values, a matter of continued and persistent faith in the child, faith that needed no evidence of change to support it. Perhaps the personal being of the teacher touched off something within the child that made the difference and opened new paths of healthy relatedness to life. Something of a miracle has occurred and the child described as delinquent suddenly becomes a responsible citizen. The miracle is that the child recovers his real self at the moment when the school principal sees him as a hopeless troublemaker. The recovery comes dramatically through being loved, not through increments of progress and achievement.

To maintain one's conviction in the inherent potentiality for goodness in the child is to stand positively behind the child's present striving for growth, perhaps when he wants and needs encouragement most. When the child's growth has been stifled, when he has become static or is moving along a path of destructiveness, perhaps someone's deep belief in him as a potentially positive person is all that is required to initiate a process of positive change.

In the process of discussion, Miss Whet seems to respond affirmatively to suggestions which would help the "predelinquent" child. Her initially strong conviction that a hostile and destructive child in her school is doomed to delinquency changes to one of hope and promise and leads to other perceptions of the potentials of even severely disturbed children.

Permitting Children To Express Their Feelings

One evening, the teachers focused on ways of helping children to express their feelings. The discussion begins with the topic of how children can be helped to express themselves in the classroom. As it continues, the teachers state their own experiences. They question the purpose and value of open expression of feelings. The excerpt below illustrates this process.

Miss Shawn: I've been thinking about starting some group approaches. Should I wait until we have some ideas from you as to how you would like us to proceed?

Mr. Moustakas: No. If you have any idea at all, I think it's most important that you go ahead and try it.

Miss Shawn: I had thought I would make available a number of things and let the children decide what they want to do. Or is it better to start out with a definite plan to stimulate children to express their feelings?

Mr. Moustakas: Whichever you feel is most fitting in your particular situation.

Miss Shawn: Some would do one thing and some other things. I could move around and be with one child or with a small group.

Mr. Moustakas: I think that has possibilities.

Mrs. Dase: Should we state the principles we are using to explain our particular approach?

Mr. Moustakas: That's up to you.

Mrs. Allen: Could you tell us what the purpose is in these activities?

Mr. Moustakas: I think there may be many purposes. One, might be to give children an opportunity to express themselves in a free, accepting atmosphere. Let's take the illustration mentioned earlier, the child who drew a picture of the devil. If in the total context of the classroom and the specific process of the drawing the teacher could have put herself in the child's place she might have understood the feeling involved.

Mrs. Dase: As I see it then, we're not working with the group to solve specific problems but to provide a situation where children may express their experiences. Is that true?

Mr. Moustakas: Yes, that could be the aim. It is possible, however, that a specific situation upsets the group as a whole and creates a problem. Then the teacher might provide a time when this particular problem could be discussed by the children.

Miss Whet: Generally when I've tried that a small number of children do most of the talking.

Mr. Moustakas: Yet a large number may actually be participating. (Pause). There is nothing wrong in focusing more on some children than on others.

Mrs. Hoch: What if children say things that you don't regard as being important.

Mr. Moustakas: Then I don't think it's necessary to make a response. If the child says, as a simple statement of condition, "I'm wearing a brown sweater today," no special response is needed, but if he shouts this angrily it may be important to explore further with him the basis for his feeling. Children's fantasies, daydreams, imaginations, fears, and angers may all have a special significance to the child. But it's important that the teacher respond in a spontaneous manner and not stop and think about what she *should* say.

Mrs. Cone: I started something in my class. I asked the group what they liked about school and what they didn't like. I wrote all of their feelings down. We decided every Monday afternoon for an hour and a half we'd discuss these feelings. There were some children who didn't want this talking-over period so they are bringing things from home to work on instead.

Mrs. Bairn: This morning I told my group of fifth grade children they could talk about anything they wished, good things, bad things, things they liked and didn't like. What came out were nice happy things, nothing bad, no problems.

Mr. Moustakas: Do you think the only time a discussion has value is when there are problems?

Mrs. Bairn: No but I was surprised. I expected something very different. If I keep this up will their fears come out later?

Mr. Moustakas: If the children feel safe in discussing fears they probably will.

Miss Tars: In our Weekly Reader there was an article on a new anesthetic. This was my opening. I asked my group if anyone had been given ether in the hospital. All hands went up. You could feel the tension rise. Nearly every child had a hospital experience he wanted to tell. I just listened. The discussion continued for an hour and a half. Two told about very serious operations, the removal of a tumor and an eye.

Miss Whet: My whole class was upset this morning. They had read the story in the newspapers of the mother who had killed her baby. They couldn't understand why she would do it. They talked about this for almost an hour.

Mrs. Bairn: I saw an instance of a mother attempting to

teach her child, who was four or five, not to bite a neighboring child. She bit him to show him how it hurt.

Mrs. Sall: Two wrongs don't make a right.

Mr. James: We had to do the same thing in our house and it did make it right. One of the girls when she became upset started to fight and would bite so we just bit her back and she stopped.

Mr. Frank: There's a question that's bothering me. Think of all the people in each of our communities who never had a chance to talk over their feelings with anyone. They grow up into people like we are. What happens to their fears and hostilities?

Mrs. Long: But think if we had the opportunity how much better we might all feel.

Mrs. Sall: Most of us have had different ways of releasing our feelings as we grew up.

Mrs. Wull: I think when we grow up and harbor hostilities and resentments, jealousies, or envies, they hurt us more than anyone else. We'll keep trying to find some way to change.

Mr. Frank: But it may take a long time to find out the kind of person you really are.

Mrs. Dase: Don't we all know it from the inside?

Miss Whet: I don't know about my anxieties if I have any.

Mrs. Wull: You must know when you've hurt or damaged someone. When you are free and happy then the whole world is right but when you destroy another person you also destroy yourself. On days when we've done something wrong, we can't help but reflect upon it. It bothers us and the sooner we can do something to make it right our thinking is better off and we are free inside to do our work.

Mr. Frank: But if I just think about this person who uses poor judgment with her child and makes him suffer, if I just think about it, I feel stormy inside.

Mrs. Dase: A little hostile yourself?

Mr. Frank: And I can't do my work or even digest my food right.

Mrs. Sall: Is it necessary to always do something to relieve hostility? It seems to me with grown-ups sometimes conditions change and the hostility dissipates on its own.

Miss Tars: Yes, I've had that feeling. I can get in a bad mood and be really upset. I don't know why. I'll try to think why but I don't know. After a while I get out of it. I think in time the feeling dissipates but you have to learn to live with yourself again.

Mrs. Dase: If you can handle these feelings and be free of them, you can do a better job with the children and all people.

Mrs. Cone: To get back to our groups. I feel free in my present situation to try out some new things but a lot depends on your principal.

Mrs. Sall: When I first started teaching I had a lot of enthusiasm about what I wanted to do. But the principal would walk in and stare at me. I felt he disapproved of everything I was doing. It made me so nervous I was afraid I couldn't go on. I stopped using my own ideas and began teaching from the teachers' manuals.

Mrs. Dase: I felt that way too. It wouldn't bother me now.

Mrs. Sall: It all depends on your principal. Some are so critical of everything. No matter what you do it turns out to be wrong.

Mrs. Cone: Yes, it all depends on their attitude.

Mrs. Dase: You can tell too by the way they look at you.

Miss Dean: If you know they are critical of you, you are bound to be tied up in knots.

Miss Morse: They can make you feel their authority over you.

Comments

This discussion shows the instructor's response to teachers' questions. He actively encourages teachers to experiment in the classroom and try out group approaches which fit their own situations. His comments convey his valuing of spontaneous inventiveness in encouraging children to express their real feelings. He suggests that the teacher sometimes can initiate a discussion which focuses on problem areas which seem to be affecting many children in school and that expression of feelings can be of value even when there is no problem involved.

At first, there is much verbal exchange between the instructor and the teachers but as the group begins to explore their own thoughts and feelings, the instructor participates as a listener. The teachers discuss the value of open expression of feelings in facilitating growth, harmony, and happiness in living.

Mrs. Cone brings the group back to the classroom situation and stresses the importance of having support from the principal. Others briefly express their experiences with principals. All seem to feel that acceptance from the principal does much to free the teacher to experiment and to discover meaningful ways of relating with children in the classroom.

References

1. Commission on Teacher Education. *Teachers For Our Times*. Washington, D. C.: American Council on Education, 1944.
2. Dewey, John. *Democracy and Education*. New York: The Macmillan Co., 1916.
3. Rasey, Marie, and Menge, J. W. *What We Learn from Children*. New York: Harper & Brothers, 1956.

THE TEACHER'S EXPRESSION OF SELF
IN RELATIONS WITH PARENTS

Relations between teachers and parents show an unusual paradox. Parents are viewed both as a chief threat of the teacher and as a significant resource. Teachers seek and appreciate the information and skill which parents possess but are threatened with their ideas, plans and evaluations. Teachers often express their hostility and resentment, as well as their dependence on the support and friendship of parents. Some of the negative feelings and attitudes lessen in intensity as teachers explore their relations with parents, as teachers have an opportunity to see themselves, and understand the nature of their involvement. Sometimes a clear perception of the issue or conflict occurs and a change in attitude results. As the teacher talks, different aspects of a total experience enter the relationship. In every case, there is an emotional release felt by the teacher. When he is understood and supported by other teachers, he is open to positive and healthy contacts with parents.

A number of illustrations have been selected to point to the teacher's expression of self in parent relations and to show how this expressive process leads to understanding and personal growth.

I

Mrs. Hoch: I've often found it true that it's the parents with the best adjusted children who ask for conferences with the teacher. The ones who really need them never ask.

Mrs. Long: I don't understand. Why is that?

Mrs. Hoch: They're afraid to come in.

Miss Whet: They don't want to face the facts.

Mrs. Hoch: I think parents influence children in security. Some children aren't very conscious of their differences until mothers say, "Why are you doing that?" The child in school usually accepts his shortcomings but it's the parents you hear from. It may not be the parent's fault in all instances but in a great many it's the parent who makes the child feel insecure.

Miss Whet: Parents should be told what they are doing.

Mrs. Long: But don't you think that when parents make their children insecure they know it and feel badly?

Miss Whet: Yes, but I want them to feel worse.

Mrs. Allen: I have a little boy in my class from Oregon. He was put in the second grade and then put back after a month. He was fine the first number of days in the first grade. Then his mother came and told me what a bad child he was at home. He threw his food on the floor and whined a lot. She said it right in front of him. She kept saying he should be in the second grade. The mother earlier had agreed that he belonged in the first grade.

Miss Shawn: That isn't the story she told me. She said you offered her a choice but made her feel that only one decision was possible.

Mrs. Allen: She said she didn't want to make the decision. So I told her I could be a benevolent dictator and put the child in the first grade. She seemed satisfied at the time.

Miss Shawn: Yes, but it still had a disturbing effect upon her.

Mrs. Allen: She insists that psychologically the child would be a failure all the rest of his life. She has instilled in the child's mind now that being in the first grade is a terrible thing. Now he keeps telling me: "I don't belong in the first grade. I belong in the second grade." He's so mixed up he doesn't even know my name. He calls me teacher. He fits in well with children in the first grade. In fact, last week when we finished one of the primers I asked him if he wouldn't like to take it home and read to his folks and he said, "Oh they know I can read. They think I'm a good reader. Why do I want to take it home and read to them?" He wouldn't take the book home because he knows he can't read it, because that's what his parents think of him. So he didn't take the book home and I asked him again today and he said no, that he didn't want to be bothered. So I said, "Well all right, if your parents know you can read and I know you can read so we'll just forget about it." But the trouble is he can't read well and he knows it. He knows there are children in the first grade that can read better than he does. How can ordinary teachers reach parents like that?

Mrs. Long: I think teachers are too anxious with parents. They think they can do it in one conference and change parents' attitudes overnight. We want to work miracles.

Mrs. Allen: It's understandable. We don't want children to continue to be damaged. She thought it would affect him the rest of his life and that he never would be normal because he was put back and she was so sorry that they had ever come out here. She wished she'd stayed in Oregon. Then she finally, when I pinned her right down to it, started discussing his first grade. He had had three teachers. One had had a nervous breakdown and all showed he passed on condition. So if he would have stayed in Oregon, he wouldn't have been in second grade when the second grade teacher tested him to find out where he belonged.

Mrs. Sall: The parent doesn't realize that the grade the child is in isn't the important thing. It's the kind of growth he's achieving.

Mrs. Cone: I had a situation not long ago with a father. He came to me positive that his son was much too smart to be in the third grade with other children his age. The boy was very intelligent, interested in science and scientific experiments. I tried to tell him even though he was in the third grade, mostly he was working on matters on an individual basis but he needed companionship with children his own age. I never did convince the father.

Mrs. Dase: I think we've done a lot to make parents feel guilty. I've tried awfully hard. I've come to learn from talking with parents not to have them feel badly and guilty. For example, if they have only one child, we must accept this and not blame everything he does on the fact that he's an only child. It's a highly personal matter. Maybe there are good reasons if there is only one child. Sometimes they will come in and sit down— I don't ask any questions at all—and sometimes they'll say: "I suppose you think all his trouble is due to the fact that he's an only child." And I'll say, "Don't apologize for his being an only child." And it's amazing how much more comfortable they feel when someone says the child's problem is not due to his being an only child.

Comments

During this discussion a number of parental failures are pointed out by the teachers: Parents are afraid to face the facts; parents who most need conferences fail to come for them; parents make children aware of their shortcomings;

parents make children feel that failure in school is a terrible personal defeat; and parents do not realize that the child's growth is more important than his grade level. With regard to teachers' failures, it was stated: Teachers try to work miracles; teachers expect too much of parents; teachers are too anxious with parents; and teachers force parents to act against their own wishes and convictions.

Many facets of parent-teacher relations are explored by the teachers. Although some are quick to see the shortcomings of parents, others relate teachers' misunderstandings and irresponsible behavior. Those who looked at specific parents as hopeless and interfering reconsidered their relations and saw possibilities for initiating positive approaches. The teachers realized that they must accept the realities of the parents' life and try to understand and respect the parents' point of view.

II

Mr. Frank: I have a problem that is very current. This boy has—there are two children in the family, a second grader and a fourth grader. I think all the trouble started a year ago. Maybe I should say that the children lack self-discipline. A year ago last September the boy in the fourth grade stood up on the partitions in the lavatory and fell on the floor and cracked his skull. I mention this as one of the kinds of things he does in school. Before this there was a neighborhood fight. This is background which may be pertinent. There was a neighborhood fight between three families. It didn't concern the school especially until it got into fights between home and school among the children of the mothers who were not getting along. Then it was a great concern of mine. I talked with Mrs. Long about it. Asked her if she would come in. I never knew how brave I am until this incident. I invited those three mothers to come in. I had a telephone call that night. The husband of one of them, (the father of the child I'm speaking of) said, "What are you doing?" and I said, "Well, the neighborhood fight doesn't concern me but when it gets in the school then it is my concern. I have invited the three principals in the case to come in and I invited our Mrs. Long who is pretty good at this sort of thing to come in." He said, "You are a brave man." That's when I found out I am brave. He said "I will have my wife there if I have to drag her there." These were his words. She was there.

I bought some cookies and made a pot of hot water and got some tea bags. We met in the cafeteria. Mrs. Long will never forget this either. This was quite a deal because these mothers were almost to the point of attacking each other right there. Everytime it seemed to be boiling up to that level, I poured more tea. I reached in front of them, like this, and poured tea. Mrs. Long put in her quieting kind of comment and we avoided open warfare. Anyway toward the end of the thing, things came along, and there was some understanding and some tolerance of each other. We made another date for the following week. Mrs. Long played the big part but the tea played a role in it. The children are still undisciplined but the mothers are doing better. A couple of weeks ago I happened to teach in the room where the boy is. I had to continually bring this boy back to his work and remind him not to bother the ones around him. The whole time I was there I was continually bringing him back to his place. On one occasion when I wasn't in the building he came tearing into the building and running through the hall. He was apprehended and taken to the office. Hands were laid on. One hand was laid on once, not nearly so hard as if I had done it. Incidentally I have done it. Immediately, the mother was upset and referred to the person who administered the spat as "that woman." She said, "She is a public servant and what do you do to a person who works for you that you don't like." She answered her own question, "You fire them. That's what you do and that's what I'm going to do." I said, "If you could do such a thing, none of us would stay in teaching." She had no objection to me administering corporal punishment, but "That woman can't do it." She added that her boy was tried and convicted without any evidence. She is at the point now of threatening me with her husband. I think maybe I'm going to have another conversation with him. His reaction before was everything that I could ask for. The boy was told that he should not come to school early at the same time the corporal punishment was administered. There was a bit of objection to that but they are going to let that one go by. Yesterday she called me and asked me what I had done about the spanking and what I intended to do. I said I thought her good judgment would have come to the fore and her anger would have cooled. But she hadn't changed any. She said, "I will come to school today with him and I will sit in his room as his guard. If no one else will help, I'll take care of him." I said, "You may come in as a visitor. Parents are always welcome as visitors. However, you will not be in charge of the room and you may not come as a guard." Before she called me she called Dr. Nelson.

Miss Morse: What did she expect him to do?

Mr. Frank: Fire the teacher.

Mrs. Long: I know this mother. I think she's so confused with her own personal problems she doesn't know how to get along with people. She's pretty unhappy.

Mr. Frank: I've talked awfully straight to her and she never becomes angry with me.

Mrs. Long: She recognizes the problem, I believe. Maybe she's getting to the place where she would be willing to do something about it.

Mr. Frank: The last thing I would want is punishment for her. I have concern for her kids only.

Mrs. Sall: Do you think it would help her if she visited other rooms and saw the problems there? She might be able to understand how irritations can mount and anger the teacher.

Mr. Frank: I don't know. (Pause). She doesn't resent corporal punishment as long as it comes from a man.

Mrs. Dase: Do you approve of your teachers giving corporal punishment?

Mr. Frank: I abide by the administrative manual which says any laying on of hands shall be immediately reported to the principal and to the superintendent of schools in writing. When it's done in good judgment, then I back the teacher.

Miss Whet: Did the teacher really give him a walloping or just a slap?

Mr. Frank: Just one, on the pants.

Miss Shawn: Was the boy very upset?

Mr. Frank: I've known him for several years now and I don't think he was.

Miss Whet: It seems to me she made a big issue of something very minor.

Mrs. Dase: Do you think you can rely on authority to settle this problem? Couldn't you approach her with the attitude, "We want you to understand we all feel positively about this youngster and want to help. We both have our feelings about the incident." Then maybe she wouldn't have to defend herself against the authority she so fears.

Mr. Frank: Yes, that will be my approach when she comes in again.

Mrs. Hoch: Are you trying to help this woman or stop her from putting pressure on the teacher?

Mr. Frank: I'm trying to stop the pressure on the teacher as that affects the children too. As for any other kind of help that is not my responsibility. That's for a psychiatrist to handle.

Mrs. Long: Apparently this hits some very strong sensitive area in her and she's not able to drop it.

Mr. Frank: I feel she thinks she must go on to some kind of showdown.

Mrs. Dase: Isn't it possible that this mother feels very threatened over what's happened and from her point of view the only way of protecting herself is to resist the situation. There was no acceptance of her resistance so all she could do was resist more. What I'm saying is that I can understand how she could become more resentful and angry.

Mr. Frank: You think what she did was right?

Mrs. Dase: No, but understandable.

Mr. Frank: Yes, I see what you mean.

Miss Morse: I have a situation of a parent and child who need help. The parent came to me before I went to her. I did what I thought was right according to my values and also professionally or ethically right to the best of my knowledge. I found she completely took what I said to her and rearranged it and made it into something that I didn't say and didn't mean. She went to other people who are higher up and tried to turn them against me. I wasn't in trouble for it. I hadn't done anything to get me into trouble. She took the wrong way. Then she came back to me. I pretended I didn't know anything about it. It was very hard. It was against my—it was very difficult for me. It is getting more difficult because everytime—I really dislike seeing her now. She comes often. I know everytime I see her it is just going to create something more. You don't feel yourself.

Mr. Moustakas: You are trying to keep your personal feeling out of it and act professionally but it is very hard.

Miss Morse: I'm afraid to say anything further to her because it may be misinterpreted. Yet I feel talking with her is the only way we can settle this difficulty.

Comments

This session further illustrates how the expression of real experience is itself a process through which understanding and personal growth are achieved. Mr. Frank explores with the group the problem of facing a hostile mother. He starts by reporting and defending his rejection of the mother but as other teachers enter the discussion he begins to see his own involvement, and to respect the mother's position. He realizes the problem cannot be settled arbitrarily and through authority. He emerges from this experience with a positive view for relating with the mother.

Miss Morse expresses the nature of her relationship with a deceitful mother, the hopelessness of the relation and her bitter feelings toward the mother. As she expresses this experience, suddenly she realizes that "talking with her is the only way we can settle this difficulty."

III

Mr. James: I have a problem that I would like some help on here. I'm having lunch tomorrow in the office with one of the fathers. There are four children. The oldest is my concern. She's about one year back of the group. She's a very sweet little girl but she doesn't like school. She doesn't like Sunday School either and says, "Five days are enough." The father sent a note, saying he didn't like the idea of the school not helping her work up to grade level. From her record I learned that every year since the first grade she's been about one grade level behind. It has been my thought that maybe she should go back to the fourth grade where she could make a very respectable place for herself. She certainly wouldn't be obvious. She's small for her age. The mother was sure the father wouldn't approve. I can make this decision no matter what the father says. Would it be wise to put her back in the fourth grade?

Mrs. Long: Did she repeat a grade before?

Mr. James: No. She has never repeated a grade. She's been a grade behind all the way. I'm especially concerned because she's so unhappy and dislikes school.

Mrs. Dase: I would think she'd be just twice as unhappy if you put her back now.

Mrs. Walk: How come she's never been retained before?

Mr. James: That's what her father is going to ask me tomorrow.

Mrs. Walk: She should have been held back in the first or second grade. I think it's too late now.

Mrs. Dase: Well, to me, putting her back would add to her problems. She would be in a daze suddenly to find herself with forty new children.

Mrs. Long: Have you talked with the child?

Mr. James: No, I haven't. I wouldn't talk to the child about this. Any child would say No. That's not the way to approach it.

Mrs. Dase: If the child's been unhappy all this time, she's not going to be any happier in the fourth grade.

Mr. James: Maybe I've given a false impression. I wouldn't say the child has been unhappy all the time. I really don't know.

Mrs. Walk: Wouldn't you think it would be better for her to take the fifth grade over than to move her back in the middle of the year? I think it's bad for a child suddenly to be removed from her group.

Mr. James: Well, she's not going to like it any better in June than in January.

Mrs. Long: Is she doing failing work in the fifth grade?

Mrs. James: She's doing fourth grade work in the fifth grade.

Mrs. Dase: Is that why she doesn't like school?

Mr. James: She doesn't like school because she doesn't have a respectable position scholastically in the group.

Mrs. Dase: She'd feel worse in the fourth grade. She'd feel she'd really been labeled.

Mr. Downs: Why has her school record been mediocre all these years?

Mr. James: I don't think it's been mediocre at all. She's made a year's progress every year.

Miss Shawn: What about special help outside of school, such as tutoring? Maybe over a period of time she'd make up the grade.

Mr. James: Yes, that's a possibility.

Miss Shawn: Has she ever had outside help?

Mr. James: No, she hasn't.

Miss Shawn: I had a similar child once with whom I couldn't spend the time he needed. I recommended tutoring. Well now, in the fifth grade, he tops the class in reading. He had about two years of tutoring and he is very proud of his accomplishment. It came from inside. He really felt he wanted to read better.

Mrs. Allen: I have this child in my room who is not adjusting at all. He's doing his work all right now but he failed last year. The first thing his mother asked me: "Is he failing again?" "No," I said, "He isn't failing but he isn't adjusting to school." She said, "He worries all Sunday afternoon about coming to school because he hates school." She wants to talk with me about a private school. Before I meet with her I'm wondering what I should say about his going to private school. I feel she needs to talk to someone else who can tell her the advantages and disadvantages of private school. (Pause). He's a miserable child. He bounces into school and can't sit still. He crawls around. I feel he's very, very disturbed and I feel unable to help him. I think he's not getting anywhere with me.

Mrs. Bairn: Does your principal know about this boy?

Mrs. Allen: Yes, I think so.

Mrs. Bairn: I always call the principal when a parent is coming in. Why don't you handle it your own way, though, because you know her and know how she feels.

Mrs. Allen: I think I'd rather go through the usual channels but I don't think this mother would want to talk to the principal.

Mrs. Bairn: Yes, sometimes they feel fearful about going to the principal but usually they are willing to talk with him.

Mrs. Allen: I don't know. (Pause). He is very, very disturbed and unhappy. I have three of them and they shouldn't be together. They just irritate each other and fight constantly. Yet they can't stay away from each other. I try to keep them apart but they're at each other every minute.

Miss Whet: Don't you think a lot of it is caused by the home situation?

Mrs. Allen: It certainly is. Another strange thing about him is that he's very, very polite with guests. Then, he is personality plus. He brings the chair out and asks them if there's anything he can do. It's really obnoxious to me to see him behave that way. Because he's just the opposite kind of person.

Mrs. Cone: Last year this boy was in my room. I know what Mrs. Allen means. I had a couple of high school students practice teaching. They came in the room and by the end of the day, they were so fascinated by Willis. They just hated to leave him. They thought he was the sweetest and cutest little boy. He was. The minute they walked in he went up and introduced himself and got them chairs, kept explaining what he was doing. He doesn't do a thing all day. They thought he was the nicest child in the whole room. Then I had him going to this reading teacher, the supervisor for reading, and she said, "Oh, he is the greatest little boy, and he has the keenest little mind." He knows all about cadets and all that sort of thing. But as far as anything in school goes, he can't sit still. He's all over the room all day long. The little things that amuse him. He'd go on the playground and he wouldn't play with any children. He'd always gather up the little stones and gravel. Then he'd come in and say, "Because I love you so much, Mrs. Cone, you can have any color of stone you want." And he'd sit there all day and roll his stones on his desk while he was supposed to be doing his work. (Laughter). He'd push one, then he'd push another. He wasn't interested in school. I don't know what his trouble is. I had the mother in for two or three conferences. Willis was outside the building the first time and she went out and got him. She sent her daughter out. She said, "I want you to sit here and listen to everything that Mrs. Cone has to say." So I didn't feel like saying much in front of him. To the few things I did say, she said, "You want me to tell your father that. You want me to go home and tell your father that. You know what he'll do if I tell your father." She said, "If he acts up once more at school or at home I will tell his father."

Mrs. Long: He is really a problem and something has to be done.

Mrs. Dase: I think he needs a good, solid, firm friendship with some outstanding person in the room.

Mrs. Allen: The outstanding ones don't want to have anything to do with him. You know that birds of a feather flock together and that's what's happening in the room. I think he needs a firm, consistent discipline. That's what he's getting from me.

Miss Shawn: Then what good would private school be?

Mrs. Allen: I don't think she can push off her responsibility by putting him into a private school. I had a boy who was in a school with only seven others in his class.

I think that was part of his trouble. He had too much attention and wouldn't do anything at all. He had to be constantly reminded by the teacher. This boy is not quite like that but maybe he's never had any real responsibilities at home. He still needs to discover his potentiality and his worth.

Miss Morse: I had a child in my room for three weeks this fall and he just wasn't ready for first grade. The mother came in one day and said that her child was put ahead probationally. I didn't know that. I knew he would be much happier in kindergarten than he would in the first grade because he was so small. She said, "Well, let's think about it for a while." I said I would talk to the kindergarten teacher. So I talked to her and she suggested we get together with the mother and the mother said, "Fine, I'll take you to lunch." So she took the two of us out to lunch and we both recommended he be put back to kindergarten and she said, "Well, that's fine. That's what we'll do." They have three children and she had little conflict with the children. I mean this family is really wonderful and she told him he was going to be put back to kindergarten and he was going to be a leader in the kindergarten and that the kindergarten teacher invited him back. Not everybody gets invited back. So I didn't say anything at all to my children and none of the children said anything for about a week and then they asked me what happened. I said that the kindergarten teacher had asked him to come back and he said he'd like to go back which he did. They just forgot it. We see him in the hall now and he waves. The mother says she thinks that's the best thing. She's never regretted it. She says he's a different child this year. So there's a difference in parents. I feel if the parent is willing to help the child and you talk to them honestly about what would benefit the child, they respond.

Mrs. Long: I wonder how much we as school people can take a certain responsibility for going a second level with these kids and making it unnecessary for mothers to show aggravated symptoms that were mentioned a while ago, this feeling and sense of resistance. Also, the fact was mentioned that she has been defeated so many times in her own personal ideas of what she wants to do to bring her youngsters up and all that sort of thing. There are many kinds of defeat and that sort of thing that she feels. One part of her personality is rising to the fore and she is going to defend her children and do the very best she can for them. We as school people look at that and say, "That doesn't look very sensible. It isn't consistent with something else." It seems to her, her behavior is completely consistent with the way she feels about life and herself. Are we going to expect the mother to change when she is not having outside clinical help and having a tremendous struggle within herself? I don't think we should put too much emphasis on the mother and see how well we can do with the youngster.

Comments

Mr. James begins this session by asking the group for help in making a decision. Though he says he has an open attitude toward the situation his comments seem to indicate defense of a particular position, that of demoting a child who for most of her school life has been one year behind grade level. None of the teachers recommend that the child be failed. But the alternatives do not satisfy Mr. James until Miss Shawn suggests the possibility of tutoring the child. Mr. James accepts this suggestion and indicates a willingness to act on it.

Mrs. Allen continues the discussion with a related problem. She, at first, seems uncertain as to how to deal with a parent's interest in placing her child in a private school. Her conclusion differs from that of the instructor and other teachers in the group who believe that the child would respond to a substantial friendship. Though her firm, consistent discipline has not been effective, her recommendation that the child "needs to discover his potentiality and his worth" contains hope for a positive school experience for the child and for change in the teacher's attitude.

Finally, a different experience with a mother is expressed, one where the parent is helpful and co-operative. Mrs. Long points out to the group that criticism of the parent only aggravates the symptoms of a child's failure and encourages further parental rejection.

The problem of failing children always brings parent and teacher together in a relation which can create problems and conflicts, or one which can result in a mutual agreement and a plan. It is clear that the parents' attitude, value, or belief cannot be ignored in the failure of a child. Consideration of the parents' viewpoint, as well as the child's, is vitally necessary to the reaching of a decision that really will contribute to the child's growth. A child who feels that failure is a terrible personal defeat, whether this is transmitted by the parent or not, bears an emotional scar that cannot help but be destructive in his school experiences. The teacher must strive to understand and accept the parent's view, however distorted or inconsistent it may seem. Rather than putting pressure on the parent the teacher must devote his energies to helping the child. This help cannot be given by finding all the answers to the child's retardation in faulty, irresponsible, and rejecting parental management.

CHAPTER 6

SPELLING CONTESTS, GRADES, PRAISE AND PUNISHMENT AND OTHER EDUCATIONAL ISSUES

Apart from the relations which influence the nature of the teacher's growth, there are a number of educational issues which deeply concern the teacher. Those frequently expressed by teachers include: academic training and character training, personal values and professional values, co-operation and competition, grades and marking, spelling contests, praise and punishment, fast and slow children, and teacher-child ratios. Given an opportunity to explore them from their own personal experience, teachers often see how these issues influence the learner. A number of examples are presented to illustrate the content of the educational issues and the teachers' growth in exploring them.

Spelling Contests

Miss Morse: Did any of you see the spelling contest last Friday? The last two were a boy and a girl. The girl spelled fast and the boy very slow. The boy won the contest.

Mr. Frank: I think many of the kids know how to spell the words they miss. I don't believe it's a contest of spelling but a test of nerves.

Mr. Downs: Also luck. If they had gotten a different word they might have stayed up until the end.

Miss Whet: The ones who could use the help in spelling are ignored. We drill and drill the ones in the top group.

Mrs. Dase: Too many of the children in spelling contests get pains in their stomachs and become ill before they are through. I don't think they're good for anyone. I'm against them.

Mr. Wann: When they get out in life they have to compete, don't they?

Mr. Frank: Not in spelling they don't.

Mr. Wann: They have to compete. When they do, that little bug still gets in the stomach.

Mrs. Allen: The same thing is true about athletics.

Mrs. Dase: I don't see any value in spelling contests.

Miss Shawn: I don't either.

Mrs. Long: I can't see any reason for having them.

Miss Whet: The teacher ends up by giving most of her attention to the few in the top group.

Mr. Frank: They're supposed to be the best spellers in the school. Our runner up is a better speller than the winner.

Miss Whet: What's the value of forcing children to compete to be at the top?

Mrs. Hoch: Some of the children who usually don't do too well in spelling pick up because of the spelling bee. They want to do better and are really interested in competing.

Miss Shawn: In our school one girl became so nervous that she was shaking all over. She had absolutely no control, became a nervous wreck. She looked like she was on the verge of an epileptic seizure. When it creates that kind of thing I—

Mrs. Sall: That's the reason I don't like it. Two of the children were sick to their stomachs in our grade bee. I tried to take the pressure off them, saying, "Only one is going to win, so don't worry about it." But you can't take that pressure off.

Mr. Wann: Isn't it true that a certain percentage of men always get sick before an athletic event? They get sick but it's worth it to them. It's their choice.

Mr. James: I think it's a good experience. I think it does a child good to be on the spot and still keep his head.

Mrs. Hoch: What about the child who is very shy and doesn't succeed in a lot of things? When he wins a spelling contest, it makes him more confident.

Mr. Frank: Those are not the one's who win.

Mrs. Hoch: I think children enjoy them. When we had them in school, we enjoyed them.

Mr. Wann: The observers are just as interested as the spellers. It's like saying, "Why have baseball?" You get excited. You get upset. Why do anything if it excites you? Excitement doesn't hurt anyone.

Mrs. Sall: If it makes you sick inside it does. If it makes a child tear up her handkerchief, be so wrought up that she stands and chews on her dress—I've seen that and I think it's very damaging.

Mr. Wann: They're going to have to face things like that in life.

Mr. James: Maybe it's good to tear up handkerchiefs when you're excited.

Mrs. Dase: Is it good to tear up your heart too?

Mrs. Hoch: I had a boy who never was a good speller but when the spelling bee came, he really tried. He worked for it and lost. He shed a few tears and he's the last person in the world to shed tears. I'll bet he'll try again. I don't think the experience hurt him at all.

Mrs. Cone: We didn't have one this year. The teachers voted against it.

Mrs. Hoch: That's not fair. You should have let the children vote on it.

Mrs. Dase: I don't agree. I think we have a right to decide how we'll teach spelling.

Mr. Wann: I saw a line of children one time lined up to get a blood test. Some of them were awfuly sick. Some passed out before they even got to the table. If we followed some of these arguments, we'd do away with blood tests.

Mr. Frank: I think that's an entirely different question. There is usually an important reason for getting a blood test. I see no real reason for emphasis on winning a spelling contest. It isn't even a test of spelling but a test of memory and nerves, mostly iron nerves.

Mrs. Hoch: I think it's a true test of spelling.

Mr. Frank: I don't agree with you. Through the years the children in our school who are the best spellers usually do not win.

Mrs. Sall: I can tell you we're going to keep having them. The biggest stockholders in the newspaper that sponsors them live in this area. If we ever tried to stop them we'd have an immediate storm of protest from these people.

Comments

There was strong feeling in the teachers' voices and an intense atmosphere during this discussion on spelling contests. With the exception of three people in the group, the teachers nodded affirmatively when Mr. Frank stated that spelling contests were tests of memory and iron nerves in the face of terrific, mounting pressures. The main support for spelling contests was that competitive experiences under pressure would help children better face the realities of life. The majority, however, believed that continuation of spelling contests indicates lack of understanding of the basic issues and values involved. The breaking down of a child's moral fibre and self-confidence with the resulting sense of shame and personal defeat is a serious matter, hardly justified by strengthening the competitive powers of the few who emerge victoriously. But majority opinion in a group does not settle an issue. The divided nature of the group was keenly felt by the members. This strong difference permeated the entire meeting without change or resolution of any kind.

Grades

Mrs. Dase: I want to say something about grades. Grades are always used to compare one person with another, never in terms of the child himself. I hate to answer the question "How does he do in relation to other children?" I suppose you have to tell parents and others to get along with them. But it seems to me that people should think of a child in terms of what he himself is doing.

Mrs. Sall: Why couldn't we just write letters home telling what the child is doing, not in comparison to anyone else.

Miss Whet: But parents seem to prefer letter grades.

Mrs. Dase: We should stand by what we believe whether parents agree or not. Some are satisfied with the grades. Some are not. We should not be willing to compare the child with others.

Mrs. Allen: Yes, but we have no choice. A survey was made here a few years ago and the majority wanted grades.

Mrs. Cone: It's the parents who demanded grades from teachers. I believe 65 per cent voted for the five-point marking system.

Mrs. Dase: We're going to continue having problems with children as long as parents insist that we compare and rate children.

Mr. Frank: But we can't just go our own way. That happened in Woodhall. There was a real blow up. The superintendent was fired. The parents wanted a marking system and the superintendent decided against it. The teachers didn't even back him up when the showdown came. It has to be done by mutual agreement.

Miss Shawn: I think it would be interesting to ask the children what they'd like.

Mrs. Allen: I have. They want A, B, C, D, E. Even the one's rated the lowest.

Mrs. Cone: Very few of the children wanted no grades at all and only about two per cent of the parents.

Miss Whet: How many here would vote for no grades at all?

(*All teachers raise hands.*)

Mrs. Dase: I have taught in a school where they did not give grades, not ever. You weren't permitted to give gold stars or anything like that. The idea was that a child would be satisfied if rewards were intrinsic to the work and not based on outside standards. Those who do not achieve feel badly and are damaged by low grades.

Mr. Wann: What about the problems he'll have to face some day in the competitive world. He'll not be paid according to his attitude but according to his ability. Children have to learn to compete. When they grow up and go out into the world and meet unfriendly competition, they aren't going to know what to do.

Mr. Moustakas: In our society, practice in competitive situations seems absolutely necessary.

Mr. Wann: In any society.

Mr. Moustakas: If we can accept reports of anthropologists, it seems that some cultures exist and thrive without competition.

Mr. Wann: It would seem to me that if we didn't have any competition, everything we have obtained would decay. There would be nothing left but rubble. No one would be concerned with growth and improvement.

Mrs. Hoch (to Mr. Moustakas): We would become primitive like the tribes you've referred to.

Mr. Moustakas: You seem to be using competition to mean the unfolding, blossoming, expanding of the individual's potentialities.

Mrs. Dase: I don't believe Einstein made his discoveries from a competitive urge.

Mrs. Long: Yes, the original ideas for invention and change come from the expansion of some individual's creative concept or plan, not from a competitive urge. It's the production of it that is competitive.

Mrs. Dase: Competition exploits the discovery. It is unnatural.

Mr. Wann: Natural because it comes from nature, survival of the fittest. Practically everything in nature is competing; one against the other in order to survive. I couldn't call competition unnatural.

Mrs. Allen: Competition is a natural part of the physical state of a person. I don't think we can ever get away from it.

Comments

The teachers unanimously agreed that if they had a choice they would do away with grading. A basic evil of grading was described as the pernicious effect of comparing children with each other. Some members of the group felt that teachers must stand by what they believe and think of the child only in terms of himself and what he is doing.

Several teachers felt that pitting one child against another developed competitive ability and helped the strong to grow and thrive. Mr. Wann assigns an encompassing value to competition, saying that without competition, everything we have obtained would decay and no one would be concerned with growth and development. Mrs. Hoch and Mrs. Allen also feel that competition is a natural, inherent part of human life, inescapable, and without which civilization would decay. Some teachers believe that true growth and discovery do not stem from competitive urges but from the exploration of an idea or plan, the fulfillment of potentiality.

The issue of whether cooperation or competition is inherent and natural to the human organism is not resolved in this group. However, the majority of teachers believe that competition is based on cultural values and conditions while cooperation is a natural impulse of human life. Though research evidence is conflicting on this point, the question remains: What does man want for himself? If he wishes to develop a spirit of cooperation among human beings everywhere, then he must stop inculcating children in the belief that competition is inevitable in social life and begin to value the growth of the cooperative attitude in all human endeavor.

Fast and Slow Children

Mrs. Cone: I have a question tonight regarding the speed with which a child completes his work. The child who is not fast only has to do ten problems in arithmetic or reading while the one who is fast does twenty.

Mr. Frank: Which one are you concerned with, the child who does only ten or the one who works fast and does twenty?

Mrs. Cone: Sometimes the child who does twenty feels that he is being imposed upon. One child for instance was letter perfect in everything he did but terrifically slow. I feel he just didn't have the kind of personality that goes fast. I think he will always be that way. He never quite finishes. I don't think it is right for me to pressure him to do more. How can we explain that to the ones who finish their work?

Mrs. Sall: I have the same situation. It never seems to bother the youngsters. Everything Bobby does is letter perfect but he finishes only about half the assignments. No one complains about it. I don't think you need explain it.

Mrs. Dase: If you don't make an issue of it I don't think they are concerned with what a child is doing or not doing.

Mrs. Long: We have to let these children work at their own pace. If you rush them they'll get discouraged and get more and more behind.

Miss Shawn: Yes, I think it is good enough if he can go on on his own.

Mr. Frank: I had a situation like that two or three years ago. A boy who is now in high school. This boy, you couldn't speed him up any more than his own natural gait. His mother was a very highly nervous individual, fast. She snapped into anything just like this. She was very concerned about it. He was slow at home and slow at school. He was a swell kid. I thought a lot of him, and his teachers did too. She was the one who was very concerned about him because he didn't snap around like she did. I didn't know the father and I said, "Is this boy like the father?" and she said, "Yes." I suggested to her that the father had made a pretty good place for himself in this world and probably the boy would too.

Comments

Here the value of allowing children to work at their own pace is explored. Each teacher recognizes that children differ in the rate at which they work. Acceptance of the unique pace of the child is a necessary requirement in the learning situation. In this discussion, the group does not refer to the use of competitive goals and rewards in urging children to work more rapidly. There is consensus that the natural pace is the child's own pace, and this must be respected as an inherent quality of the child's pattern of growth.

Punishment

Mrs. Allen: Last Wednesday afternoon at recess a child bit another one. I think it should have been handled right then and there.

Mr. Moustakas: The child should be punished on the spot?

Mrs. Allen: Well, he certainly should know that his behavior is not acceptable.

Miss Shawn: It seems to me if you punish the child for a destructive habit you wouldn't be accepting the child at all.

Mrs. Allen: I think he should have been asked right then and there why he bit the child.

Miss Whet: I think he should have been made to realize that biting is not acceptable behavior for human beings.

Mrs. Long: It is harder to accept a child that harms another child than one who is just acting and disturbing but not harming.

Mrs. Allen: Didn't you ever hear it's always best not to punish a child when you are angry.

Mr. Frank: How else can you do it, except when you are angry? If I were very rational, I'd think of other things to do.

Mrs. Dase: I read an article last week entitled, "Should you spank a child when you are angry?" The article advised that you should because it is a cold, heartless thing if you wait until you are calm.

Mrs. Allen: I don't agree with that. Spanking is a form of

punishment. The child shouldn't feel that you are angry because then it is a battle between you and the child.

Mr. Frank: Yes, but shouldn't the child know that you are angry?

Mrs. Long: Well, I suppose he should know that what he has done has angered you—what he did, not him. That you still love him but he did something he shouldn't have.

Mrs. Dase: I could no more wait, but I'm thinking of my child at home, and then say in a weak way, "It is now time for me to spank you." It just wouldn't work out, I couldn't do it.

Mr. Frank: I wanted to say that on an occasion when I did not administer a spanking my dignity was outraged by the child and what he said to me. I can be a dictator in my domain. I told him to come back later and I would take care of him. We're friends now maybe because he didn't come back that day. He said he was never coming back if he *had* to come back. (Pause). Another time, a boy in the second grade took a nickel away from a smaller girl. He was a good sized boy. I asked him why he did it and all he kept saying was, "I wanted it." I got a fifth grader to waylay him and take his milk money (which I got back to him later) to teach him how it felt. I did it because I tried everything else and got nowhere.

Mrs. Sall: Was he told it was a put-up job afterwards?

Mr. Frank: No, he wasn't.

Miss Whet: I had a child last year who spoke very mean to the children. I often felt I'd like the things done to him that he did to others. But I felt that would be wrong. There is always something in the child that makes him act the way he does. I just wanted badly for him to get that same feeling even when I knew he couldn't help himself.

Mrs. Dase: I think people have already hurt him perhaps in ways you don't realize. If you encourage others to retaliate I think it will only make him worse.

Mrs. Wull: There is an expression that when you are most unlovable you need love most.

Mr. James: It's very hard to love someone who mistreats you.

Mrs. Allen: You can turn the other cheek.

Mrs. Long: No, that's a form of rejection, ignoring the child.

Mr. Frank: I tried to tell the child who stole the nickel how it feels but he ignored everything I said. I could think of no other way.

Mrs. Sall: Actually you were training him to keep out of trouble.

Mrs. Dase: Yes, but also to be happy.

Mr. Frank: It seems to me that a human being has to learn to avoid certain things because of the consequences. But I'm asking would there have been a better way? (Long pause).

Mrs. Dase: It seems to me you treated the symptom not the cause. You haven't eliminated the attitude that made him want to attack the girl in the first place.

Mr. Frank: I had to do something. I couldn't let it go.

Mrs. Dase: I'm not condemning that. I can see where you had to do something, but as you said, you didn't think it solved the real problem.

Comments

In this session the teachers do not reach a decision on how to approach and manage in a healthy way the child who attacks and hurts others. Some state retaliation is often used but all agree that this method sometimes does more harm than good. Another issue was whether punishing the child on the spot and in anger is a sound method or whether waiting before punishing results in a better solution. No conclusion is reached by the group nor is there consensus on a satisfactory principle.

If the teacher is truly interested in the child's growth she will not destroy his sense of self. If a child must be punished, it must be done in such a way that the child is able to maintain his dignity and self-respect. When the integrity of the child is attacked or violated he is forced to defend himself and withdraw or find some way of retaliating.

Praise

Mrs. Cone: I would say that through praise you might change the individual's attitude toward his work.

Mr. Moustakas: Have you found that to be true?

Mrs. Allen: I was told that if you praise the child when it is genuine praise, it will affect the child's attitude.

Mr. Moustakas: Don't you think that what is good work will be felt and perceived as good by the individual?

Mrs. Cone: I don't think people realize too often how well they've done. Somehow they have a feeling that what they are doing is not good, yet it actually can be.

Mr. Moustakas: Then you believe that attitudes of worthlessness are changed through praise.

Mrs. Cone: Don't you believe that's true?

Mr. Moustakas: I believe that satisfaction is experienced from within and rewards are intrinsic to the child's direct experience.

Mrs. Cone: But are you discouraging any kind of remark?

Mr. Moustakas: I do not believe that all remarks have to be evaluations.

Mrs. Allen: Then you are opposed to giving a child gold stars when they do exceptional work?

Mr. Moustakas: Yes, I am. But remember this is based on my own experience. This is me, not you. You may find it's worthwhile, that it has an important place in the classroom and then I would say, "By all means continue it." But as I see it, too often in such a situation work is done to please or for some other external reward, not for an inner sense of satisfaction. Too many children learn to behave on the expectations of others. When they make a tree or house, it has to be just exactly as it appears. They soon are unable to draw or paint as they feel. When this happens I think something very basic is missing, the freedom to express one's potentiality in some medium without the pressures of records and outside standards.

Comments

Some of the harmful effects of praise on the development of the child's potentialities and sense of value are briefly discussed in this session. It is an example of how the instructor presents his own beliefs, pointing to what may have been a different orientation for some teachers. He, at the same time, encourages the teacher to maintain his own convictions and methods of relating to children as long as these approaches prove meaningful and beneficial for teacher and child.

CHAPTER 7

A RETURN TO THE SELF:
MRS. ALLEN'S EXPERIENCE

Mrs. Allen entered the group determined to have the instructor present a series of lectures on mental health. For many meetings she persisted with this request. She wanted to be told how to solve problems, how to locate causes of children's disturbing behavior, what techniques to use to get children to act as they should. At the same time, she told others what was wrong with their teaching, gave exact advice, and specified particular ways of solving various educational issues and difficulties with children, parents, other teachers, and administrators. During the early meetings she frequently remained at the end of the sessions to criticize the instructor, to state her dissatisfaction with the class, to stress that the instructor was confusing instead of clarifying, and to indicate that other teachers in the group needed direct help from the instructor to become better teachers. She felt there were many damaging teachers in the school system who needed to be evaluated and weeded out. She was persistently aggressive in trying to influence the instructor to behave in accordance with her beliefs and values.

The instructor encouraged Mrs. Allen to be critical, to state her feelings openly, to stand by her ways of teaching and her sense of the appropriate and the right in teaching.

He did not often agree with her or change his behavior to satisfy her requirements but he tried to express his feeling that her way was worthy for her and that because it came out of her own experience it was meaningful and understandable. Often, in the beginning meetings, other teachers were critical of Mrs. Allen but the instructor always supported her, with a feeling of acceptance and a desire to know her in her own terms.

For a number of meetings following the initially explosive period, Mrs. Allen maintained a stony silence, mixed with frequent gestures of anger and disgust. Then she became deeply involved in a relationship with one child in her classroom. This experience opened new pathways of relatedness for Mrs. Allen. She began again to remain after class to talk with the instructor. She asked many questions, usually not waiting for a response, but continuing to express certain vital experiences with the child. At this time, she became accepting in her relations with other teachers. She seemed to be listening with complete attention to the experience of others. She was undergoing a rather basic transformation away from the previously narrow, and relatively closed orientation, toward an open, exploratory attitude. She was able to speak in the specific, concrete terms of her own experience rather than in sweeping generalizations. She stopped imposing her standards and values onto others. She seemed for the first time to accept the uniqueness of each teaching situation and often even to support other teachers and encourage them to express more fully their own vital experiences, however different they were from her own. She began wholeheartedly to trust members of the group and to speak freely and confidently.

Briefly, Mrs. Allen changed from a cold, objective, and external view of relations to a warm, human, subjective regard for others. When she became personally involved and humanly committed, she could permit her real self to be expressed. She could trust the validity of her own self-integrations and allow the personal to become real in her relations. She became alive and growing as a person.

BEGINNING OF THE YEAR EXCERPTS

1. Relationships With Parents

The nature of Mrs. Allen's relations with parents is reflected in the following excerpts.

1. As a person working with children, I feel more strongly all the time that a parent can do little to help with the actions of their children. They can't understand the feelings and children's experience.

Comment: Here Mrs. Allen shows her lack of regard for the parent as a sensitive, understanding person. She states that parents are unable to manage their children's behavior. The underlying feeling seems to be that teachers can expect little or no help from parents in dealing with children's behavior in a constructive way.

2. Mrs. Allen: I have a little boy in my class from Oregon. He was put in the second grade and then put back after a month. He was fine the first number of days in the first grade. Then his mother came and told me what a bad child he was at home. He threw his food on the floor and whined a lot. She said it right in front of him. She kept saying he should be in the second grade. The mother earlier had agreed that he belonged in the first grade.

Miss Shawn: That isn't the story she told me. She said you offered her a choice but made her feel that only one decision was possible.

Mrs. Allen: She said she didn't want to make the decision. So I told her I could be a benevolent dictator and put the child in the first grade. She seemed satisfied at the time.

Miss Shawn: Yes, but it still had a disturbing effect upon her.

Mrs. Allen: She insists tht psychologically the child would be a failure all the rest of his life. She has instilled in the child's mind now that being in the first grade is a terrible thing. Now he keeps telling me: "I don't belong in the first grade. I belong in the second grade." He's so mixed up he doesn't even know my name. He calls me teacher. He fits in well with children in the first grade. In fact, last week when we finished one of the primers I asked him if he wouldn't like to take it home and read to his folks and he said, "Oh they know I can read. They think I'm a good reader. Why do I want to take it home and read to them?" He wouldn't take the book home because he knows he can't read it because that's what his parents think of him. So he didn't take the book home and I asked him again today and he said no, that he didn't want to be bothered. So I said well all right, if your parents know you can read and I know you can read so we'll just forget about it. But the trouble is he can't read well and he knows it. He knows there are children in the first grade that can read better than he does.

Comment: Mrs. Allen presents the problem of demotion in such a way that the parent is unable to make a decision. She recognizes the authoritarian nature of her relationship with the parent but justifies her action as that of a "benevolent dictator." Mrs. Allen places the responsibility for the child's difficulty onto the mother. She implies that the mother's hopeless attitude has caused the child's school failure. She points out that parents refuse to face up to their own shortcomings. By being afraid to face the facts, according to Mrs. Allen, parents contribute to children's anxiety and sense of inadequacy. She feels that parents make their children feel rejected by making them conscious of their objectionable ways.

3. Then she finally, when I pinned her right down to it, started discussing his first grade. He had had three teachers. One had had a nervous breakdown and all showed

he passed on condition. So if he would have stayed in Oregon, he wouldn't have been in second grade when the second grade teacher tested him to find out where he belonged.

Comment: Mrs. Allen shows how she succeeded in getting a mother to admit that her child had been a school failure. She indicates how truth can be arrived at through pressure and by pinning the parent "right down to it."

4. These older parents often go along with a child and do his thinking for him and don't give the child a chance to learn to take care of himself.

Comment: Here Mrs. Allen makes special reference to older parents. She finds them particularly over-protective and feels they make their children dependent, and keep them from being able to think and act on their own.

5. I don't think she can push off her responsibility by putting him into a private school.

Comment: Again, Mrs. Allen states her feeling that parents are irresponsible and avoid the facing of reality.

Summary

Mrs. Allen in these early meetings of the seminar expressed her belief that parents can do little to help the teacher in managing difficult children or in understanding children's feelings and experiences. She stated that parents refused to face up to their own shortcomings, were afraid to face the facts, and contributed to their children's sense of anxiety and inadequacy. She regarded older parents as over-protective of their children. Her approach to parents often was an attempt to force them to admit their poor judgment and failure and to recognize their distorted view of a situation.

2. Relationships With Children

The brief excerpts below point to the nature of Mrs. Allen's relations with children during the early meetings.

1. What if you can't work out a relationship. Isn't it best to transfer the child. . . . Maybe he's beyond our help. Maybe we'd do him a service to send him to another school.

Comment: Here Mrs. Allen conveys her belief that the child should be transferred if the teacher isn't able to work out a relationship. She does not recognize the possibility that removal of a child from the group might be experienced as a kind of absolute rejection by the child and may severely stifle his striving for self-realization.

2. I think he should be asked right then and there why he did it. He certainly should know that his behavior is not acceptable. . . . Didn't you ever hear it's always best not to punish a child when you are angry. The child shouldn't feel that you are angry because then it is a battle between you and the child.

Comment: Mrs. Allen feels that when children are destructive they should be punished on the spot and made to feel the teacher's disapproval. The criticism or rebuke must be expressed without any feeling of anger and in an objective way. Otherwise, the teacher encourages the child to battle with her.

3. I was told that if you praise the child when it is genuine it will affect the child's attitude. . . . Then are you opposed to giving gold stars when they do exceptional work?

Comment: Mrs. Allen finds it difficult to accept the idea that praise can be harmful, i.e., restricting and limiting to a child. She feels that giving gold stars for exceptional work is a natural or genuine expression which affects the child's behavior in positive ways.

4. I have this child in my room who is not adjusting at all. He's doing his work all right now but he failed last year. He's a miserable child. He bounces into school and can't sit still. He crawls around. I think he's not getting anywhere with me.

Comment: Here Mrs. Allen expresses her valuing of goal-direction and achievement. She does not feel the child is getting anywhere with her. She sees the child as non-adjusting and immature. It does not seem important to her that the child, who had failed the previous year, is completing his school work. She presents the child primarily as a liability. She implies that when a child is not getting enough out of a situation, i.e., not achieving or producing adequately, he is better off elsewhere.

5. He's very, very disturbed and unhappy. I have three of them and they shouldn't be together. . . . Another strange thing about him is that he's very, very polite with guests. Then he's personality plus. It's really obnoxious to see him behave that way. The outstanding ones don't want to have anything to do with him. You know birds of a feather flock together and that's what's happening in the room. I think he needs a firm, constant discipline. That's what he's getting from me.

Comment: Mrs. Allen makes a further analysis of the child and supports her view with the observation that the important children in the room do not care to relate to the child. She is concerned with the child's *need* as derived from her own standards rather than with the child's *wishes* and *interests* and his way of growing. She defends her "firm, constant discipline," saying that this is the kind of treatment the child needs.

6. All day long there's a steady stream of complaints about him. When I correct him, which is all day long, he becomes very sullen and angry, does everything I tell him not to, and speaks out against me. I just discipline him all the more, send him out into the hall or to the principal who

spanks him, and I take away his recess periods and other privileges. The only thing that keeps me going is that I'll only have to put up with him until June.

Comment: Here Mrs. Allen seems to be saying that her method of discipline is failing to achieve a positive influence on the child. However, having made this observation, she is unable to see the significance of her own emotional involvement. She comforts herself with the knowledge that she will have to endure the child only until the end of the school year. This is what keeps her going in the face of his growing antagonism and hostility. Somehow she does not recognize that the increasing aggression and rebellion of the child is to some extent a reflection of her relationship with him, a matter of the child maintaining his integrity through defiance, and not solely the result of a personal disturbance.

7. He is almost unbearable to have in the classroom. He ruins everything. He pesters, bothers, hits and teases all the time. He is very rude, impudent, loudly showing off, seems to resent everything I say as personal punishment. At first I tried to ignore his unpleasantness and gave him constructive suggestions but this did no good at all. He is one of the very few children I just can't like.

Comment: As Mrs. Allen further analyzes the child she sees him as increasingly destructive. He hits and teases *all the time* and ruins *everything*. Having offered the child "constructive" suggestions which he rejects, Mrs. Allen feels she has exhausted all possibilities. She does not realize that her own rejection of the child, in ignoring his unpleasantness, in not facing him directly, openly, honestly, in not caring about his wants and wishes, causes him to reject her suggestions which he perceives as another sign of her rejection and disapproval of him.

8. I did my best to overlook his rudeness but one day I lost all control and slapped him. I felt ill. I had never done that before.

Comment: Here Mrs. Allen conveys one aspect of the final breakdown in her relationship with the child. Slapping the child causes her to feel ill and deeply disturbed. It is the only time in these early meetings that she verbally expresses any personal concern, anxiety, or questioning of her treatment of children in her classroom.

Summary

Mrs. Allen indicates that when the teacher fails to work out a relationship with a child, the child should be transferred to another school. She believes transfer is also appropriate when the child fails to achieve or produce. Mrs. Allen recommends that children be punished on the spot and be made to feel the teacher's disapproval. The punishment should be administered without any feelings of anger and in an objective way. She feels that gold stars and similar rewards always have a positive affect on the child's behavior. In conveying the nature of her relation with individual children, Mrs. Allen sees one child as "miserable," another as "very, very disturbed and unhappy," and a third child as "sullen and angry." She concludes that outstanding individuals in the group do not want to have anything to do with the "obnoxious" ones. When a child ignores the teacher's punishment, further discipline and removal of privileges are necessary. She describes her relation with a child who is unbearable to have in the classroom and tells of her dislike for him. Finally, she mentions losing control and slapping a child who has been extremely rude to her.

3. Relationships With Teachers

The brief excerpts below express the nature of Mrs. Allen's relationships with teachers at the beginning of the year.

1. The problem of teachers allowing children freedom

is with the children making too much noise. . . . When a teacher gives children freedom, she should consider all the other teachers around her.

2. Teachers should give children plenty of practice in competitive situations. . . . Competition is a natural part of the physical state. I don't think we can ever get away from it.

3. It's the teacher's responsibility to cover the subject matter of the year. She can do it in a pleasant way but if she fails to do her job then the next teacher must work twice as hard.

4. We should fail children who are not doing the work.

5. The new teacher will have to follow the practices of her building or she'll find herself very, very unhappy.

Comment: Mrs. Allen's remarks with reference to other teachers are mainly in the form of directions and impositions of her own preferences and needs. She announces that teachers should plan for competitive experiences in their classrooms, should cover the syllabus of subject matter for the year, should fail children who are not completing assignments, and should follow the practices of others in the school. She cautions other teachers about giving children freedom in the classroom, warns that noisy children are a nuisance to everyone in the school, and discourages teachers from initiating new practices or procedures in a traditional or established setting.

Concluding Comments

In these comments of Mrs. Allen there is frequent use of "should" and "should not"—the imposition of a set of needs, concepts, and attitudes onto others. Her relationship with children is rejecting in nature. She expresses a belittling attitude toward parents, and conveys an authoritarian tone in her comments to other teachers. Rarely do her comments stem from personal conviction, value, and experience but rather from professional needs and from a tendency to generalize, to state choice as fact, and to appeal to the word of the expert.

Mrs. Allen's expressions are very different in the later meetings. Excerpts have been taken from these meetings which show her growing sensitivity, acceptance, and regard for parents, children, and other teachers.

END-OF-THE-YEAR EXCERPTS

1. Relationships With Children

The excerpts below convey the nature of Mrs. Allen's relationships with children at the end of the year.

1. I am afraid to form opinions of children too quickly and perhaps do more harm than good. It takes time to develop a good relationship. . . . When I learn of the situations affecting a child's behavior, I marvel that he acts as normal as he does.

Comment: Here Mrs. Allen, in her own personal terms, recognizes the value of allowing a relationship to grow in its own time, not hurrying or pressuring its character but letting positive experiences accumulate. She realizes the importance of understanding the meaning of the child's perceptions as well as the special circumstances and conditions which exist in his background of personal experience. She is concerned not with history but with the immediate reality of the child's life.

2. I have found that it takes quite a while for a child to accept a teacher as a friend when his past experiences with adults have been unpleasant. One cannot force the desired acceptance—always it must come from the child.

Comment: Again, Mrs. Allen shows respect for the child's background of experience and recognizes the importance of understanding the child in his own terms. She points to the necessity of relating to the child as a person of absolute integrity and of allowing him to come to positive attitudes in his own way and time.

3. Each child is different and must be handled differently. . . . Each child should feel wanted in the group and take his place but he should be accepted as he is. . . . Each child has value regardless of his destructive behavior or inability to learn.

Comment: Mrs. Allen comes to value each child as an individual and expresses her belief that the child must always be considered as a unique person. She indicates that group participation and social acceptance are important but only when the individual is accepted as he is. She has come to believe that each child has potentialities for self-fulfillment regardless of previous experience or background, and no matter how severe the learning handicap. Again, Mrs. Allen shows her respect for the individual and his special background of experience. There is an underlying recognition of the importance of relating to the concrete individual, not on the basis of mass instruction and technique, but in terms of personal interaction.

4. I now believe it is best to work with a child naturally and not try to push my way into his thoughts and feelings. I feel I have done some pushing and this has resulted in relationships unsatisfactory to me.

Comment: Mrs. Allen refers to her own change in attitude. She now deplores the harm which comes from pressuring or forcing children to conform or behave in ways unnatural to their own self-direction and growth. She feels dissatisfaction in probing into a child's thoughts and feelings, and in influencing him through external pressures, standards and values.

5. I made no effort to keep him in a group during work periods but allowed him to decide what he wanted to do.

Comment: Allowing the child to work out his own academic program, represents a significant change in Mrs. Allen. She did not actively encourage the child to develop his own individual interests nor did she force him to remain with the group. She simply accepted his strong wish to engage in projects of his own choosing, projects which contained an intrinsic worth for him.

6. I said nothing about his sitting on the back of his chair but insisted that he sit in the back of the room where he couldn't bother anybody.

Comment: Mrs. Allen does not permit the child to interfere with the activities of others but within limits he is free to express unacceptable behavior. Mrs. Allen does not condemn the child as socially destructive. She sets a limit simply and responds to the concrete situation without invoking a history of misdemeanors and without generalizing to the morals or character of the child.

7. We began to work things out together. I tried to anticipate some of his actions so that he could avoid trouble and find a better way. Soon he realized that I sincerely wanted to help him.

Comment: Mrs. Allen expresses her wish to be a helping person. She conveys her attempt to be sensitive to the child's varying moods and outbursts of behavior. She tries to foresee difficulties which might arise, to prevent them, and to approach the child in positive terms. Her approach is one of understanding and empathy. She focuses on positive aspects of the relationship in facilitating the child's growth. There is sensitivity and acceptance here instead of the former critical and rejecting attitude.

8. I learned he lacked necessary background to carry on his lessons during work time. So we started some private lessons after school. He soon began to catch on.

Comment: This is a further expression of Mrs. Allen's positive attitude toward the individual child. It shows a willingness to go beyond the stated requirements of a teaching schedule and to make possible the extension of an individual relation outside school hours when this is the only way.

9. John was seen all last year (by a psychiatrist) and it didn't help at all. Nothing helped until I decided that it was up to me and I began to find a place in my heart and in my teaching for John. The year is almost over and I still haven't fully succeeded with him. . . . John will emerge someday as a full human being and function according to his real potentials instead of constantly reacting to a hostile world.

Comment: Mrs. Allen expresses her belief in the child's potential for positive growth in spite of his frequent, destructive behavior. She sees only glimpses of John's real self but these glimpses mean more to Mrs. Allen than anything else in the relationship. She discovers, in this case, that outside resources are not enough. She has to find a way within herself. Whereas earlier she responded primarily to John's shortcomings, Mrs. Allen now realizes that her own attitude must change. She must find a place within her heart for John. She must begin to see and value his potentialities.

10. I told him I had enjoyed having him in my room and if he ever wanted to talk things over with me again at any time, I would be glad to listen and try to do what I could. He looked at me and said, "Would you really?" That look made a lump come into my throat.

Comment: Again, Mrs. Allen expresses an openness of attitude, an availability of self to other. She experiences a feeling of satisfaction and joy, knowing that she has been instrumental in freeing a child to discover himself. His final glance contains all that the relationship has meant to him. Is there any greater reward in teaching than to see a confused and hostile child become an alive and fully growing human being?

Summary

Mrs. Allen's end-of-the-year comments point to different attitudes in relations with children. She takes time to develop a good relationship and to understand the child. She respects and honors the child's background, however different or unhealthy his experiences may have been. She recognizes the importance of not forcing the child to trust and accept his teacher, of letting him set the pace in the relationship, on his own terms and in his own way. She permits the child freedom to engage in projects of his own choosing and accepts his choices even though they may depart from the usual classroom activities. She values group participation but only when it permits the child to express his individuality, when it is based on a truly cooperative spirit. She wants to help the individual child and is willing to see him after school if this is the only way to develop a relationship. Finally, she looks for the strengths and potentialities of the child whereas earlier in the year she saw only the limitations.

2. Relationships With Parents

During the end-of-the-year discussions, Mrs. Allen referred to parents only twice. Even so, these excerpts are significant in that they convey something of the changing nature of her relations with parents.

1. For one thing I'm really anxious to meet his father and see the way he feels about it. I wouldn't think of failing Jim but I'd like to get some help from his parents.

Comment: Earlier, Mrs. Allen regarded parents as interferers. She did not feel they could contribute to the resolution or clarification of a problem. In the above instance she welcomes the father's view. She fully expects to be helped by a parent rather than be criticized or blocked.

2. I never had any contact with her unless I called to tell her of some new misdemeanor which involved Larry. Now both parents come to our PTA meetings, take part in other school functions and really try to cooperate. Larry and his parents were not the only ones to change. I think the great-

est change of all came about in my own thinking when I at last realized that Larry was a unique person who would never conform to the ways of others and that his parents had to be accepted and sympathized with rather than blamed.

Comment: Mrs. Allen relates the changing nature of her relations with Larry and his parents. The more she tries to force Larry to conform, the greater is his resistance. Mrs. Allen comes to respect his individuality and to see his parents in a new light. Positive attitudes have emerged toward these parents. There is a feeling of sympathy and acceptance instead of blame. A cooperative relation has developed and parents and teacher work together in the interest of the child's growth.

3. Relationships With Teachers

The nature of Mrs. Allen's relationships with teachers at the end of the year is conveyed in the excerpts below.

1. I know just how Marian feels. I wouldn't want to stir my principal. . . . I understand just what you mean. Some of you have suggested that we take positive action but I say each of us has to work out his own salvation.

Comment: Mrs. Allen for the first time during the year understands the feelings of another teacher and offers her support. She states her position in personal terms, as an expression of her own experience rather than as a generalization or imposition. She accepts the fact that others may act in a different manner. She feels that each person must come to his own way of facing difficulties in interpersonal relations.

2. A teacher must help a child grow in his personal behavior as well as in scholastics. . . . The basic three R's which we were hired to teach seem secondary when children are unhappy.

Comment: This attitude is in contrast to Mrs. Allen's

earlier position that the teacher's primary responsibility is to teach subject matter. Here she expresses the belief that the child's personal experience, his feelings and attitudes, arc of crucial importance. She feels that the teacher must help the child to be happy and to develop as a person.

3. Teachers need to find a place for every child. Some children try all our patience, ingenuity and resourcefulness yet there must be some way for us to reach every child.

Comment: This is Mrs. Allen's way of saying that the teacher must respect the individuality of each child and honor it by being unreservedly committed to helping the child realize his potentiality regardless of the difficulties involved. Finding a place for each child means acceptance of the child's self not as theoretical premise but as personal conviction.

4. The teacher must express to him that she is aware of him as a person and wishes to help him.

Comment: Mrs. Allen believes that the teacher must make known her perception of the child as an individual, her support of him as a person, and her wish to be an enabling person in the child's exploration of interests and potentials and resolution of difficulties.

5. I believe a teacher must be sensitive to the actions of a child and know when to be gentle and when to be firm in each situation.

Comment: Mrs. Allen earlier in the year stated only the restrictions, the rules which cover classroom misdemeanors and the ways to punish the child to get him to behave in a socially acceptable manner. Her perception of justice and fairness was to give an equal measure of punishment for each destructive act. In the above expression, she has come to see the significance of understanding the total situation, the meaning it holds, the child's attitudes, and the pressures which induce him to behave as he does. She does not eliminate limits in her current thinking. She becomes gentle or firm in terms of what she feels is required by the child in the course of his growth in immediate situations rather than by setting prior standards and trying to stamp out objectionable behavior on the basis of these standards.

6. I think teachers must have faith in children and help them to become acceptable members of society through understanding and encouragement.

Comment: This attitude is very different from Mrs. Allen's earlier expressions. She substitutes faith, understanding, and encouragement for formal instruction, on-the-spot punishment, and group pressure. Here she wants children to become *acceptable* members of society whereas earlier she spoke of the need for children to become *conforming* members of society.

7. My teaching has become a little too definite. This class has made me feel this all year long. Now I'm starting back to the way I wanted to teach when I left college. I feel relieved and understand what has been bothering me the last four years—I have not been free to teach on the basis of choice and conviction.

Comment: Here Mrs. Allen points to the changing nature of her attitude. Actually there is not so much a change as a calling forth of her real self, earlier feelings and attitudes which she feels to be consistent with the kind of person she is and wants to be. Something has been bothering her in her four years of teaching—her denial of self, her departure from personal virtue, from being, from acting on the basis of choice and conviction.

Summary of the Nature of Mrs. Allen's Relationship With Other Teachers

Mrs. Allen, in her end-of-the-year statements, conveys the different nature of her relations with other teachers, away from dictating and imposing and toward acceptance and respect. Many of her expressions begin with an attitude of "I believe," "I feel," or "I know" rather than "You should" or "Everyone should." She states that each teacher has to work out his own salvation. She believes that each teacher must recognize and be concerned with the child as a self-consistent, whole person and not solely with the child's achievement in school subjects. When the child's happiness and self-fulfillment are threatened, everything else is secondary. She feels that teachers can find a way of reaching each child, however severe the handicap or destructive the behavior. She feels that the teacher must let the child know she is aware of him as a person and wishes to help him. She believes that if teachers have faith in children they can help children to become acceptable members of society. She recognizes the rigidity of her own teaching, her inward rejection of prescribed standards and roles, and her desire to return to being a teacher who is self-involved and who teaches on the basis of choice and conviction.

Conclusion

From Mrs. Allen's expressions of experience early in the year it is possible to see her as a teacher who attempts to influence children, parents, and other teachers through absolute requirements and standards, an exclusive devotion to subject matter, a contempt for individuality, uniqueness and difference, a rejecting and punitive approach, and an imposing, authoritative, hostile manner. It is possible to see authority as the central theme in her behavior and freedom and openness consistently absent. From excerpts at the end of the year one can see the respect for the individual, the valuing of the personal in teaching, the desire to bring happiness and self-fulfillment to children, the belief that personal growth involves the individual discovering his own way, the acceptance of differences, and the importance of faith, encouragement, understanding, and openness of attitude in personal relationships. Perhaps these two perceptions of Mrs. Allen represent differences, rather than changes or a personal transformation. Mrs. Allen herself indicates a return to a real self and self-consistency, a recovery of something already within, something existing as value but temporarily dormant and denied. Perhaps the intrinsic self appeared when Mrs. Allen could express an external self in an atmopshere of acceptance and trust, in a situation where she was free to express and explore her own beliefs, values, and experiences. She removed the distortions, the self-imposed restrictions, the "shoulds" and restraining limits, and got back to the roots of her own personal experience, and the spontaneity, warmth and humanness which made her work worthwhile and brought again substance and meaning to her life.

Chapter 8

THE TEACHER BECOMES A LEARNER

The teacher is responsible initially for creating a structure in which the vital experiences of learners may be fully expressed. Within this structure, a process of expression of the real self begins. He sees essential meanings within different classroom situations and arrives at insights which help him to continue to grow, insights which also become occasions for the growth of others. The teacher must be fully himself to free others to be. He must encourage the development of an open, exploratory attitude in the learner.

In the situation which is a true occasion for learning, the teacher also becomes a learner. He cannot enable another person to grow unless the process he initiates also makes it possible for him to learn. He learns from listening, in the full human sense, to the vital and significant experiences of each individual in his group. He learns to be open to each expression of the learner and to discover within each situation its unique and special qualities. Within the context of a concrete living situation, the teacher comes to understand the nature of a particular person's experience. It is in the particular experience that potential insights and dynamics exist.

The teacher must listen, with all his being, to grasp the meanings and values within the learner's experience. He must relate himself to another's experience and come to know the other as a unique person. He must come to understand the dynamics of personal situations through listening and experiencing, as fully as he can, the expression of those most deeply involved in these situations.

Frequently within the experience of the teacher certain class meetings have a special significance, a wholeness and moving quality, which excite the teacher and make him want to see more clearly the feeling-insights which are in the process of developing. If the process is a creative one, in the act of expressing himself, the teacher sees patterns and relations that had been only partially understood; that is, he comes to realizations that go beyond his specific experience in the classroom.

The teacher must find some form of expression which allows his experience to flow and take him where it will. He has just experienced something very basic which he cannot really understand until he attempts to express it. He knows there is something he must express to arrive at the meaning or insight he is searching for. He lets himself, what exists within as some vague totality, emerge until he has said all there is to say. He stops at that point where he fulfills his growing potential in some immediate experience.

To illustrate this process of the teacher's expression of self, a number of examples are presented. These illustrations are taken from notes written immediately after sessions with the group of teachers appearing throughout the book. Sometimes tape recordings of the class meetings were used but usually the writer proceeded immediately to express his experience.

I

Tonight it suddenly occurred to me, as I was speaking of something else, that groups of children often do not need an adult to guide their learning. I had just visited a school where most children in the group were deeply absorbed in self-chosen activities. I had seen the teacher devote herself on this afternoon to three individual children. It did not occur to me at the time that this was unusual. But this evening as I expressed to the class my valuing their own self-chosen activities in a mental health program, the words simply came out. I began relating my experience of the afternoon. I found myself saying that most often children do not need or want a teacher. When they are truly themselves, they become absorbed in projects and are unaware even of the teacher's presence. The notion that the teacher must spend a fair and just amount of time with each child seems like a mechanical response to external demands rather than to the immediate situation. What travesty to measure the value of a personal relationship in terms of time. For one child, all that is required is an exchange of glances, an exchange which has great significance for both teacher and child and makes all that follows worth while. Another child requires the full personal presence of the teacher throughout most of the morning. Only to the impersonal observer of these situations is there an important time difference. In experience, being is timeless. Teacher and child are not related to time but only to each other.

Another malevolence in scheduling time with children in equal or fair amounts is the viewing of children as comparable, treating them as if their wants and requirements were alike, blocking the possibility of spontaneous experiences and ignoring the non-commensurable and unique nature of the individual child.

In addition to the fact that the being experience is timeless and non-comparable some children are so involved in their own projects, with a clear sense of knowing what they are about, that the teacher, trying to fairly apportion his talents, gets in the way. When the child is really involved in a process of self-education, the teacher's guidance is often unnecessary.

Tonight I tried to say to the group that often individual

children *do* need or want the teacher to be with them as they are involved in school activities and as they express personal feelings and experiences, that these are children for whom the teacher may create specific opportunities for growth.

It occurs to me that when a group of children always need equal amounts of the teacher, the teacher has made himself so keenly felt, so necessary, that children have become dependent and unfree.

Sometimes the teacher is criticized by parents and others when he devotes himself to a particular child who is having difficulties. There is the cry that individual guidance occurs at the expense of the group. Yet in an atmosphere of love members of a group are nourished and strengthened when they pool their resources to come to the aid of an individual. In the loving family, the ill child receives support from all members of the family—even when the illness is a lengthy one. There is no question but that children and parents who deeply care will utilize their resources to support the one who is suffering.

There are crises in the classroom too. The attitude of the teacher and the group toward the child who is needy or troubled can do much to help the individual live through a personal disaster or it can further impoverish the person and intensify his anguish.

The person who nourishes and strengthens another, or frees another person to be, grows in human relatedness and empathy for he comes to touch in a deep and rare way the living experience of another human being. When the teacher enters into such a relationship with an individual a fresh new world of human experience opens which enables the teacher to extend his understanding and appreciation of the meaning of individual life under varied and complex conditions.

Mrs. Sall had much to say during this evening. She mentioned that many children select constructive activities on their own and do not want the teacher while a few children seem lost, confused, or afraid and need the teacher's guidance. She felt that an egocentric attitude caused some teachers to feel that they were necessary to each child's learning. She said it often upset teachers when children learned on their own or when they learned even when they weren't concentrating or paying attention to the instruction. This seems a significant insight to me, that the teacher is threatened by the idea that learners can often learn entirely on their own and do not need or want teachers to guide or instruct them.

II

I have often wondered how a teacher who started as a strict disciplinarian changed his attitude toward learning, whether such a change could occur suddenly or required a long period of reorganization. Tonight, after the class meeting, Mrs. Cone related her own dramatic transformation. She started her first year of teaching with a democratic spirit and a belief in the potentials of learners for self-direction. Within the first month, her principal and supervisor strongly reprimanded her for trying to give children opportunities in the classroom for self-development. She was told that establishing relations with children was not her function, that she must stop wasting her time and begin to teach the subject matter for which she was hired. She began to change her teaching approach, thinking that her teacher-training background was perhaps idealistic and not consistent with the demands of a large school system. Before the end of this first year, Mrs. Cone became a well-ordered, well-organized classroom teacher who learned to employ effective means for motivating children to do the academic assignments she had planned for them. At the end of her second year of teaching her principal used her to point to as the most improved teacher in the school. He explained to other teachers how through proper supervision she had become skillful in getting children to do their assignments. Mrs. Cone began to believe that this change in her teaching philosophy was a sign of her growth as a teacher.

Then she said something that was of much significance to me. All the while she was being praised by her principal and supervisor, while she was coming to see the results of being strict and directive with children, something inside her was rebelling, something she could not clearly explain to me, but a deep feeling of utter misery that took the joy out of every glorious achievement.

Her third year of teaching was a repetition of the first two with successful results but personal conflict. Then, in the fourth year, she was given a special assignment as a reward for her success in teaching. Her job was to teach a group of second graders, twenty exceptionally bright children, a group without behavior problems and of superior intelligence. Her main task was to give them proper stimulation. As it turned out, after the first two weeks of school, she was asked to take the worst behavior problem in the school. It was in her relationship with Ronald that Mrs. Cone came to understand the process of true and vital learning. He helped her to become herself and to express what she had always felt, faith in the child's potentials for self-growth and self-direction.

Though Mrs. Cone was successful in stimulating the bright children, she failed completely when she tried to direct Ronald. He succeeded, however, in helping her to become herself. Every effort to challenge Ronald was met with antagonism and rebuke. Finally, completely discouraged, Mrs. Cone could do nothing but leave Ronald to his own ways. Much to her surprise, he began to bring materials from home, devoting lengthy periods of time to the investigation of volcanoes and volcanic activity, rock formation, land and water surfaces, and other geographic and geologic interests. Ronald brought a stone collection to school and told how he discovered the stones in different mountain regions.

Mrs. Cone began to see that Ronald's rebellion was against external, imposed standard and authority. Occasionally he made shrieking noises, ran around the room, and climbed on furniture, but mostly he worked alone or talked with Mrs. Cone of his unusual interests. Soon she came to value Ronald and the zest and excitement he brought into the group. She saw the richness of self-education and began to encourage other children in her group to develop their own special interests. In a major sense, she stopped directing classroom activities and making suggestions. Mrs. Cone believed the single relationship with Ronald helped her to be the kind of teacher she wanted to be. She began to express what she had felt to be true, that the teacher can be *an occasion* for a child's learning, but cannot determine for him what he will learn, whether he will learn, or when he will learn.

III

Mrs. Bairn startled the class tonight and helped me to see how disturbing the word "love" can be for teachers. She had just had a moving experience with one of her children. She came into our group late and began talking immediately. Elaine, a lonely and forlorn child whom Mrs. Bairn had tried to befriend, without success, approached her with a photograph. She handed Mrs. Bairn the picture of her brother Gary, whom she talked about every day, and said, "Isn't it beautiful?" Mrs. Bairn responded immediately, putting her arm around Elaine and saying, "But Elaine, it's you I love, not Gary." Elaine began to cry and uttered, "But everyone loves Gary." Mrs. Bairn held her close, repeating, "But I love you." There was a period of silence as teacher and child stood together. Then for the first time in their relationship Elaine showed some valuing of herself. She took another photo from her pocket and handed it, hesitantly, to her teacher. Mrs. Bairn responded warmly and enthusiastically, "This is wonderful, Elaine. Can I put it on the board so everyone can see how fortunate we are in having you with us?" Mrs. Bairn did not feel that Elaine's basic problem had been solved in this one encounter but a beginning had been made.

While I responded to the significance of the single incident in changing the nature of a relationship, others in the group were more concerned about using the word "love" in the classroom. The strong reaction of the group struck me. A number felt that telling the child he was liked was appropriate but to say that one loved a child would be misinterpreted. Others criticized the use of "love" as an expression of sentimentality and out of place in the classroom. Some felt a pat on the back or a warm look was sufficient. One teacher was definite in her conviction that for some children verbalizing the attitude made it a meaningful experience. There were points when the discussion became intense and heated with several teachers talking at once. It became clear to me that love is not a comfortable word for teachers.

IV

I saw tonight how difficult it is for teachers not to teach the stereotyped forms of behaving. Miss Tars started the discussion asking what she could do about children who were not putting enough content in their drawings. She was currently worried about a kindergarten child who, after two months of school, was not putting windows in her houses. Miss Tars wanted the group to help her teach the child the proper way to draw a house.

I thought of my own daughter who recently, on her first day with a kindergarten group, had experienced the lonely terror of being told that her drawings "needed to have the coloring inside the lines." Tragically enough, other children were her teachers. My daughter felt ashamed and inferior in this situation. I took an affirmative stand, believing that simple acceptance was not enough, and realizing that some values had to be actively supported. I told her how much I liked her drawings because they were her own and not drawn within narrow lines. I added that they didn't have to be like everyone else's. If she were satisfied with them that was all that mattered. When the social-educational situation seems to be oblivious to creativity, i.e. to an individual way of expression, I see the place of active support as a supplement to acceptance and a listening attitude.

Though Miss Tars kept saying she needed suggestions for teaching content, most teachers in this group urged her to allow children to draw as they wanted and felt, not in accordance with the way things appeared. An interesting experiment was described by one of the teachers. She had asked the children to draw pictures of their parents at the beginning of the year and again at the end of the year. In the first drawing many children omitted important parts of the face but at the end of the year it was rare not to have all the details accurately portrayed. The children had learned on their own; some perhaps because the learning had not become an issue or an educational requirement but had developed as a real expression of self-interest.

V

The value of the immediate living situation was impressed upon me tonight. The discussion started with several members of the group telling how difficult it was to get children to express feelings. A number of teachers indicated ways in which they tried artificially to create situations which would encourage children to express themselves. These attempts had frequently failed. Then Miss Shawn, with a beam, said, "This is not something you plan or pre-arrange. It just happens. If you see it at the time, you see it. If you don't let children express themselves when there is a natural situation, they do not want to recreate their feelings later. A few weeks ago one of my girls came into the room and in panic screamed that her barn was on fire, the one which housed her horse. The entire group became upset. I tried to stop the tide of feelings from coming out. I realized later that I was afraid to let their fears be expressed. I tried to get the group interested in something else. Finally, I ordered the children to begin an arithmetic assignment. I had stopped the spontaneous expression but there was an underlying tension in the group which lasted several days. Then, yesterday, I "recreated" the fire and asked children to express how they felt. There was little response from the group, even the child who was fully involved did not care to say anything." I can see from this situation that immanent feelings must be expressed as they are experienced. They cannot be squelched for a more appropriate time.

Later in the session, a number of teachers began to discuss the use of reports and evaluations. I have been reluctant to use an individual's past record or to make an evaluation because I feel this violates my belief in the uniqueness of each personal relationship and the incommensurable and non-comparable nature of the individual. But as the discussion proceeded I could see the need for evaluation. Mrs. Sall initiated the discussion by asking for some reaction from the group on the use of records and reports. Her own feeling was that evaluation took all the value out of relationships, that knowing about a child in evaluative terms actually interfered with knowing the child as himself. Mrs. Dase agreed, adding that when you really love a person you don't need to know anything about him. You let the relationship flow freely. Mrs. Long felt that making evaluations sometimes became necessary in order to help a child. Mrs. Walk disagreed. She felt that evaluations were a way of pressuring the child and forcing him to behave in accordance with others' standards. Mrs. Long, in elaborating her point, made it especially meaningful to me. I listened to this part of the meeting again from the tape recording.

Mrs. Long: I feel that the best relationship a teacher can have with the child is one of love and acceptance, but sometimes teachers find it difficult to feel this way toward a child. Billy, for example, is constantly in trouble in school. In some classes teachers have not developed a positive relationship with him. He frequently is punished in a way that makes him feel isolated and rejected. One day I talked to his music and gym teachers. I told them that they must treat Billy gently and with care, that the school was the place he had to be valued. I let them know that his parents were divorced and that the neighborhood rejected him severely. Other children were not permitted to play with him. The teachers hearing these things stopped punishing him and gave him more leeway in their groups.

Mrs. Dase: Yes, but their real feelings did not change toward loving Billy. What you told them made them feel afraid and guilty. You gave them an understanding which affected their behavior, but this does not necessarily lead to love and often interferes with it.

Mrs. Long: I realize that. But love is much harder to achieve in these temporary relationships. When it exists between the teacher and the child, no objective understanding is necessary. But when it does not, I find that giving just a little information or evaluation to the teacher is often enough to cause the teacher to stop mistreating the child.

Mrs. Dase: But she does so from fear and shame, not out of love.

I could see how stopping the punishment might be the

only possible change and though not good in itself—still a worth while gain.

Later this evening, I expressed my conviction that narrow structuring of a situation aimed at finding out how children feel often forced them to concentrate on parts and absorbed them in something static or past rather than in something alive and in the self. Sometimes this leads to so-called self-expression rather than expressions of the real self. The impact these comments had on the group was totally unexpected.

Mrs. Dase, started, and with much conviction, exclaimed, "Oh, yes I know. I tried to make a child aware that his frequent interruption of others was becoming more and more irritating. When he continued interrupting the group, I called his parents for a conference. They went right to work on him, making him so aware of this irritating habit that he stopped talking altogether in class. He frequently had something to say but his face reddened. He stiffened and could not talk." The discussion continued as follows:

Mrs. Hoch: I tried to make six children who constantly interrupted aware of the problem they created. Even talked to the parents as a group but it didn't help any. It made the children more aware, and embarrassed, but the interrupting continued unabated.

Mr. Wann: I know just how you feel. I had the same experience last year, the result was extremely disturbing to me. I became an authoritarian, I had to shout them down and keep them down. I didn't like myself but there was no other way I could keep them from destroying group activity.

Mrs. Hoch: That's exactly what I find myself doing all the time. It's exhausting but it's a bad element in the group. I heave a sigh of relief when the group passes on to the next grade.

Miss Tars: I have a group like that. It's just three or four boys but they are leaders and they send the group into frequent bedlam. They were that way last year too.

Mr. Wann: My group had a long history of misdemeanors too. I think when you get a group like that you're in for a miserable time.

Mrs. Dase (literally screaming): Oh no! I hate that. I disagree! When teachers talk in the lunchrooms and halls about children they are helping to create the bad reputations they despair so. I become very irked when the finger is pointed at a group. Heaven knows I've had my problems too but I can't believe that any group is hopeless. We may need extra help from guidance clinics and other sources but we must not talk about these children with sickening gestures and treat them as repulsive.

Miss Whet: But where are we going to get the help. Visiting teachers are swamped. My requests for help have been ignored. I'm not so sure anyway that these are emotional problems of the kind guidance clinics deal with.

Mrs. Allen: That's right! John was seen all last year and it didn't help at all. Nothing helped until I decided that it was up to me and I began to find a place in my heart and in my teaching for John. The year is almost over and I still haven't fully succeeded with him. He is typically and wildly self-expressive all over the place, but there are many warm, heartening expressions of the real self which keep me feeling John will emerge someday as a full human being and function according to his real potentials instead of constantly reacting to a hostile world.

Mr. Wann: When you're facing a firmly rooted set of parental and social values that reward competition and aggression, how can teachers help? I tried it last year. The parents of these children did not regard their bullying and their aggressive tactics as problems. They encouraged it as free expression. They couldn't realize that free expression is often a reaction to or reflection of values and external irritations and frustrations rather than expressions of growth potentials. I was sick all last year because I had to become the lawgiver and live with a suffering conscience. I was frequently close to a nervous breakdown. I became edgy, had frequent headaches and couldn't sleep, worrying that I was becoming a restrictive, cruel person; harming rather than helping. It was my first year of teaching here. I was alone. No one to support or listen to me. Though it didn't change my worry and guilt, it was alleviating to hear other teachers say they had tried with this group and failed too.

Mrs. Dase: I know you did your best. But you did not accept the group and because you didn't you became an authoritarian and you hated yourself for it. At least you weren't smug and self-satisfied as many teachers become when they learn others have had similar experiences.

A number of teachers shake their heads and shout "No!" Mrs. Dase's face reddens and she continues.

Mrs. Dase: I know I shouldn't say what I am but I must. I believe so strongly that saying bad things about children, believing individuals and groups to be hopeless is wrong. I think Mr. Wann failed. I very likely would have failed with the group too but I wouldn't have given up and I wouldn't have labeled the group. I'm sure there must be some way of reaching these children; if not guidance clinics or parents, through the principal. There must be some way.

Miss Whet: That may work out in your building, but not mine. The very children I've worked with the hardest, the exceptional ones in the group, are the ones I've gotten the most criticism on. A small clique of parents began gossiping that I was ruining some of the children, that I rejected them and was treating them unfairly.

How could they know that these are children I care for
the most? I've suffered with them. I know what they
go through, not only in school, but outside. Did the
principal help? No, he allowed them to talk about me
and tell of all the harmful things I was doing. They
didn't care that I was working with 42 children, that
many were not happy, that I was doing the very best I
knew how, groping, searching, trying to be a real person
with each of these children, that my wanting to be
near each child was sometimes overwhelming. They
are the same parents who are isolating Jerry in the
neighborhood, preventing their children from playing
with him and gossiping when there is nothing else
to talk about at their bridge clubs and their coffees,
morning, noon and sometimes, I think, at night. Yes,
Jerry and I were their favorite topics. Did the principal defend me—no! The worst blow of all came
at the end of their meeting when he told them:
"You've got to overlook a lot of Miss Whet's behavior.
She's new here." Well, when he told me that I could
have exploded. He had no right listening to their gossip.
What does he think a new teacher is—some sort of mental freak. I said very little, tried to explain the situation
but no one listened.

Mrs. Dase: There's where you made your mistake. You
should have exploded—told him exactly how you felt.

Mrs. Allen: I don't agree with that. I know just how Marian
feels. I wouldn't want to stir my principal.

Miss Whet: I knew why he did it. He's afraid of parents.
He's afraid they'll go to the superintendent. He's actually afraid of his job.

Mrs. Dase: Then you should have gotten the teachers together and insisted that the principal include you in any
similar conference and get the whole story.

Mrs. Allen: That may be all right for you but not for all of
us. I'm in a situation too where a few parents are mak-

ing my teaching a miserable experience and I get the brunt of it, with occasional remarks indirectly made to me by the principal.

Miss Whet: I finally called all the parents in and tried to tell them what they were doing to Jerry by isolating him, talking about him, and making him the constant object of their rebuke. Some didn't like what I said. They went straight to the principal afterwards. They weren't honest enough to express their feelings at the meeting. They waited to distort and spread what I was saying.

Mrs. Cone: How would you like it if you were suddenly told you were ruining a child?

Miss Whet (on the verge of tears): I didn't say it that way. I tried to say it kindly. But some took it as a personal attack, including the principal.

Mrs. Allen: I understand just what you mean. Some of you have suggested we take positive action but I say each of us has to work out his own salvation.

Comments

This session brought home to me in an especially forcible fashion, the unpredictable nature of the group process. This meeting turned out to be one of most significant of all. My comments touched off some basic personal experiences of the teachers, but largely of a different nature than I had anticipated. Even when the instructor attempts to direct the discussion, unless he persists, the group eventually comes to express and explore experiences which are truly vital and foremost in the minds of the individual members.

As I write these experiences, I have an overwhelming feeling of the unity and support in the group despite the strong differences expressed. The teachers seem closer to each other than ever before. It is especially wonderful to hear Miss Whet and Mrs. Allen, both of whom doubted they could express personal experiences and who distrusted those who did, discuss some of their real difficulties in relating to parents, and their relations with principals. I especially like Mrs. Allen's (who often gave advice and stressed techniques in an abstract way) coming to say that "each of us has to work out his own salvation."

CHAPTER 9

SOME OUTCOMES OF THE PROCESS OF
SELF-GROWTH IN TEACHERS

A philosophy of the self, the basic concepts and principles relative to self-being and self-education and the process through which the individual learner grows, has been discussed. Verbatim examples of the nature of expressions of the real self in various relations and on educational issues, have also been presented. Throughout the book numerous illustrations have shown the process of self-growth and some of the specific changes in feeling and thought which result when a group becomes alive and the individuals are free to openly express their significant and vital experiences. There remains in this chapter, the task of elaborating and summing up the outcomes of the growth process.

Before these outcomes are described, one digression is made to reemphasize the significance of sheer expression of self. Whenever the person sees a way of growing in a relationship, it is basic to the maintenance of self that this striving be recognized, encouraged, and valued. It does not matter whether an expression of self actually contributes or leads to change or to realization of goals. An expression of the real self must be treasured as itself, as an act of personal relating of one individual to another.

Whatever idea the individual may have for reaching others, whatever way he may perceive of moving a relationship from a numb state to one of goodness and positive strength, it must not be ignored, analyzed out of him, viewed as not worthwhile or trivial. To treat an expression of the self as weak and ineffectual is to actively weaken the self and contribute to the making of a non-self or pseudo-self. When the individual wants to give something of his own self in a relationship, the giving must be treasured and nurtured irrelevant of whether it will lead to growth and change. Unless these acts, thoughts, and perceptions of the individual are valued he cannot be an alive person. To be fully alive as a human being does not mean to be incessantly growing, but unless the person is fully alive there can be no growth. The clearest way to stifle, block, and destroy the self of the individual is to minimize his own way of seeing concrete living situations, his own way of searching for harmony and positiveness in relationships. To tell the person his type of help is not needed, his perception is distorted, his contribution is a false one, his striving for communion is illogical or trivial; to say that his gift of self is of no consequence, is nothing, is the best way to kill the growing nature of the self. We must begin with the person as he is and nurture every expression of his real self.

Only the particular teacher can live his life in a particular classroom and outside of it. No one else can do the living for him. But if the teacher is to provide occasions for the growth of learners to whom he has a dedicated responsibility then he must have a self that is substantially expressed in all his relations. However small these expressions of self may seem to others, however naive they may appear toward the solution of problems and issues, unless they have a way of coming to full fruition in a relation, the teacher cannot be truly alive. Whatever the teacher does it must stem from his own being and be valued as such or the result will be nothing at all.

The Personal Notes

One way of seeing the changes that occur in a group of learners is to ask the group to write their personal reactions to the class meetings, the feelings and thoughts which occur to them as they try to express the nature of their experience. It is important that the learner express the experience immediately after the class session so that the experience is still fresh. A number of these personal notes have been selected to convey the freedom teachers can feel in expressing their experience, the content of their thoughts and feelings and some of their changing perceptions, attitudes and ideas. The personal notes are presented as a unit though they were written by the teachers at different times during the year.

Mrs. Sall: My heart bleeds for these children who have so much to give but their mothers never see it. I've had many children whose mothers are meticulous housekeepers and where the children have to help maintain a spotless household.

Mrs. Allen: As a person working with children I feel more strongly all the time that a parent can do little to help with the actions of their children. They can't understand the feelings their children experience.

Miss Dean: I believe it's best to work with the child and do all you can do with him but keep the parent out of it as much as possible unless you know the parent and what his reactions would be.

Mrs. Walk: I have found that often in conferences with parents I'll say something to them and then wish I hadn't. They become easily upset.

Miss Whet: I shouldn't have been in school today because I was very unpleasant to be with. I don't know what can be done about it but there are days when I'm irritating and it bothers me very much. One of the children mentioned I must have gotten up on the wrong side of the bed. This is not the kind of person I want to be.

Mrs. Sall: I always leave this class with a refreshed feeling about my relationships with children. I get so tense about it all week but when we talk about different relations here I seem to unwind and feel I can start again tomorrow. I felt the discussion of children's fears very important. It helped me to better understand my own son's fears as well as those of children in my classroom.

Miss Dean: I dreaded my report tonight because I had to tell of the many incidents in which I stopped the child but I was relieved to find that the others agreed with me or at least did not disapprove.

Mrs. Dase: I enjoyed tonight's meeting especially and feel I have a better understanding of children's fears.

Mrs. Cone: I see for the first time that my children at school and at home can prize objects just for themselves or do things just for the doing. There doesn't have to be a why.

Mrs. Dase: I was impressed by the honesty in each report and the real concern expressed for the children under discussion.

Mrs. Long: I find it most intriguing to hear how people develop relations of deep feelings through a particular experience.

Mrs. Cone: I feel so sorry for Miss Whet. She seems very disturbed by her situation. I don't see how any child could learn and have a happy experience when the teacher is so tense and unhappy about the situation.

Mrs. Dase: I feel that Mrs. Allen has established a good relation with the child but is afraid to show her true feelings of affection for the child.

Miss Whet: It sometimes bothers me that Mrs. Dase dominates the class discussions and gets us off on topics primary to her but not to anyone else.

Miss Shawn: I've been wondering a great deal lately how to reach individuals whom you feel you know and understand and yet in the classroom you don't seem to be able to help them to the point they need help. I have in mind two very disturbed children who have been referred to the visiting teacher because I can't seem to give them all the attention. I want to help them and I feel I do understand them but this isn't enough. This one youngster in the last month has appeared to be burdened with so many problems that he has just gone "haywire," wetting his pants three times in three weeks, singing and mumbling to himself constantly, attaching himself to me a great deal more than before, slowing down in his reading ability. It has made me wish that the classroom teacher could do more with and for individuals. It actually hurts when you like a child and can't do enough for him.

Mrs. Wull: Oh, how can we listen to the outpourings of children and react to them when they are all relating with gusto at the same time? I can ask for one to speak at a time but then the time has gone and only one has satisfied himself. Well, maybe if I'd relate honestly to Suzie, she'd not need to pour out her experiences into my ear all the time. Then sweet Sally could be responded to, Sally who needs me but who is not aggressive.

Mrs. Dase: It is good to be in touch with a warm human philosophy with children—numbers, phonics, and marks dominate so much of the day.

Miss Shawn: It's good to get one's thoughts centered onto "with-ness" after a day of looking at academics and goal achieving.

Mr. Frank: After each meeting, I'm filled with a desire to give more of myself, try harder to understand each and every child and give whatever help I'm able to give.

Mrs. Dase: It's disturbing to me that some teachers in this group are aware of their feelings and ideas and what they want to do with children but excuse their failures on the basis of crowded conditions. I feel so strongly that the teacher must continue to live what she believes no matter what the difficulty.

Mrs. Allen: I now believe it is best to work with a child naturally and not try to push your way into his thoughts and feelings. I feel I have done some pushing and because of this the relation has turned out unsatisfactory to me. I am glad I have more time to think of how to develop a natural relation with the child.

Mrs. Allen: I have never read or heard of this method of allowing the child to experience his fears fully without encouragement and suggestion from the teacher.

Miss Tars: I felt the ideas presented tonight on expressions of the self were very foreign to me. I am very inhibited and introverted. It is very hard to feel and to express my emotions. All through my childhood my parents have been wonderful but I have been taught to hide my real feelings. Sometimes this has not been easy but my parents have always demanded it.

Mrs. Allen: My teaching has become a little too definite especially for kindergarten. This class has made me feel this all year long. Now I'm starting back to the way I wanted to teach when I left college to start my first year of work. I feel relieved and understand what has been bothering me the last four years—I have not been free to teach on the basis of choice and conviction.

Comments

A number of experiences were mentioned by teachers in their personal notes which conveyed changes in attitude.

These included the discovery that children could do things for the inherent pleasure in activity rather than for something else, that there is value in permitting children to experience fears fully without teacher direction or interpretation, and that children can be helped to grow without pressuring or pushing them. Some teachers achieved a feeling of inner relaxation and peace of mind in the class experience. They mentioned the value of the meetings in bringing them in touch with a warm human philosophy when numbers, phonics, and marks dominate so much of the day; in centering on "withness" in relationships as against looking at academics and goal achieving. They also mentioned being filled with a desire to give more of the self and to try harder to understand each and every child, and leaving the class with a refreshed and relaxed feeling after a week of many school frustrations and tensions. Many teachers referred to personal experiences in education that involved stifling, difficult relationships especially with parents and administrators, problems in passing and failing children, emotional reactions to other teachers in the group, and difficulties in helping disturbed children.

The notes mentioned frequently that the opportunity for self-exploration and open discussion in an atmosphere of acceptance and personal caring is a meaningful experience for teachers. It enables them to stop and contemplate the meaning of teaching and being a teacher. The teachers further mentioned the value of such meetings in self-growth, in bringing them to a state of communion with other teachers, in providing a source of strength, and in encouraging healthy strivings in personal relations.

The End of the Year Statement

Another way of understanding the nature of the self-growth experience is by having teachers at the end of the year express their experience in the class. This gives the learner an opportunity to look into his experience as a whole and provides data for further understanding of the outcomes. The excerpts below have been selected to illustrate the nature and value of the experience.

Miss Tars: The course has helped me to let off some steam and go back to the classroom each week with new hope and less frustration.

Mr. Wann: There was a time, about the middle of this semester, when I became very discouraged about this class, my reactions to it, and what I was getting out of it. I had heard that people who had taken this course before had changed their whole way of life because of this class. I guess I expected some dramatic change to come over me, and I was a little disappointed because I couldn't find one. I shelved this idea to think about later as I was too discouraged to think clearly at the time. Since then I have thought about it a great deal. It didn't dawn on me until I unconsciously used some of the theories we discussed in class with my own family that perhaps I had absorbed more than I thought. The change I was looking for has not come suddenly or dramatically because somehow I still cannot wholly absorb this business of completely accepting other people. I want to, because the theory is something I want to believe in.

Mrs. Dase: The "oneness" a group of teachers can feel in this type of class has been very satisfying. Most of us had similar problems, or will have, in our everyday teaching experiences, and we will feel freer in dealing with them. True learning should result in a change of behavior. I'm sure no teacher can share in the revelations of a class like this without "thinking twice" before giving the quick negative retort, sarcasm, or restrictive criticisms that make up much of the discipline of a schoolroom.

Mrs. Bairn: It was organized in such a way that it held my

undivided attention and I always left the class feeling that I had gained something worthwhile. I might add that had it not been for this course, this semester there might have been one less teacher in this world. The course came at a time when I really needed help with some of the children in my kindergarten group.

Miss Morse: This being my first teaching experience the first few weeks of school I found myself curbing my child's outward expression of behavior (contrary to the norm). This, of course, was handled in most cases in disciplinary verbal tones; such as, "We don't do that here." etc. Week by week, however, I could physically feel my mental growth through your presentations and group discussions along the road to acceptance. I know it was a revelation to me how a child can completely reverse in attitudes and actions, once he feels someone at long last knows how he feels, that she accepts him as he is. I have found this true not only with my special relationship; but also, my general attitude change has benefitted my class group as a whole.

Mrs. Cone: I thought that class discussions at first were very meaningless, because they did not seem to be on what I considered the topic at hand but it seemed to be a way of the teachers letting off steam also. However, many of our class discussions were very helpful and educational, especially those dealing with the individual child and with groups. The working with the classroom group gave me much insight on the interests, emotions, etc. of this particular group, also a foundation for planning future work and discussions with other class groups.

Miss Shawn: I have found this course very interesting. There have been several times when I have been so stimulated that I was awake way into the night, ideas revolving in my head. Much of the interest has depended upon the individuals in the class. Because these are individuals who are sincerely interested in their work, the class has been particularly interesting.

Mr. Frank: The course in Inter-personal Relationships has been of a great deal of benefit to me, much of which has been quite evident, but perhaps the greatest benefits are very intangible and hard to measure. My primary purpose in taking the course was to learn to know and understand children better, but I have found that it is in my dealings with adults (especially the teachers with whom I work) that I feel the greatest good has been accomplished. Many teachers have aggravating and nerve-wracking problems, both at school and at home, and many have no outlet for discussion of these problems. I'm sure it was frequently my tendency to brush off these irritating and tiresome recitals, to be impatient, in open disagreement, or impelled to advise. Inter-personal Relationships has given me a keen awareness of the therapeutic value of listening and fostering these discussions, aware too, that *acceptance* is more essential than agreement or advice. I find these people finishing a recital of woes with the remark, "I feel better already, just having gotten this off my chest," or "Thank you for being such a good listener." "I guess I unload all my troubles on you, just because it makes me feel better," or, "Now that I've expressed this out loud I can see where I've made some mistakes and perhaps tomorrow I'll handle this situation in a more satisfactory manner."

Mr. Downs: I'm sure I'm more aware of the children as individuals in my group. I hope in this way I have been able to help them.

Mrs. Walk: It has been said that one cannot bring anything out of an experience unless he puts something into it. I went into this course hoping to be helped in work with children and to understand them better but I came out of it with a deeper understanding of myself. The course creates a sympathetic, conscientious atmosphere which envelopes you and you just *want* to accept yourself and your children and be accepted by them.

Mrs. Sall: So many changes have taken place in the last nine months that I couldn't possibly put them all down here, but I will try to express a few. As I have attended my class this year, I have been doing a great deal of thinking about my basic beliefs and values. Many of my ideas have been strengthened or clarified. Some things have changed in value. I believe that I look at some things more objectively and see them in their true light much better than I ever did before. I look at myself and I feel that I am more aware of how others feel than I ever was before. I also express my own feelings more openly and with conviction on topics in which I believe sincerely. I have gained back my poise and belief in myself, and I am better able to stand for what I believe is right. I believe even more strongly in the goodness of human beings, and the need which individuals have for each other. Somehow I have learned some of your basic philosophy, without being conscious at the time of having learned it. This amazes me. I am better able to deal with children and their problems. I can approach the child and his problem of stealing, lying, or whatever it may be in such a way that I more easily gain the child's confidence, and I hope am better able to help the child. At least I can listen and the child can talk out his problem, no matter how badly he may think he has done. The child can get it off his mind, and with openings from me and the opportunity to think the problem through, I find that the child can come through with some very good solutions to his own problems. You were most helpful, and so were some in the class. You gave me courage to see things through, though

I had never needed that kind of personal courage before. You helped me see situations in their true light, and believe in myself again. You believed in me, and showed it in words and actions. Since your convictions were so strong, they carried weight with others, a great deal of weight. I try every day to do my best with the children, and to reach what is most vital in them. My Alex is doing very well. Occasionally he gets into trouble, but he doesn't clown all the time. I can depend on his honesty. He is so much happier. He is better liked and has some good friends in the class. The others want to help him, and he accepts their help. He takes several responsibilities. Some of the teachers have commented on his better behavior. So has the custodian. All in all I am still discovering new feelings within myself that help me to openly face my school experiences.

Comments

The outcomes of the self-exploratory experience are clearly stated in these end-of-the-year reports. Some teachers indicated that the class helped them "to let off steam," and to reach a better understanding of people, a greater awareness of feelings for children and adults, and a deeper knowledge of the individual child and the group. Others learned to listen to people without pressing or advising, but with true acceptance. The value of the experience in the development of self-discovery and personal insight was mentioned frequently. Some stated that the experience led them to develop new methods in the classroom, to a positive attitude with children, to positive approaches to classroom discipline, and to ways of helping children release their emotional tensions and move in the direction of self-growth. In brief, these statements point to new paths of relatedness inward toward self and outward toward others and a new integration or unity of the teacher's experience in school as a professional person and his personal life outside of school.

Conclusion

In an atmosphere of freedom and trust where individuals are valued, fully accepted, and respected a group of learners becomes its own best resource and serves as the primary basis for emerging insights and the resolution of problems. The instructor initially creates the atmosphere and provides the occasion for learning. Through denoting or pointing to a philosophy of self-being and self-growth, with related themes, concepts, and principles, he initiates a structure in which expression of the real self of the learner occurs, the individuality of the learner flourishes and each member of the group becomes fully alive and growing. Once the instructor completes his initial responsibility, the group functions on its own and the instructor becomes a learner.

Given this opportunity teachers are capable of deep exploration and the discovery of basic issues and underlying values, as well as related principles and facts. They develop a growing respect and empathy in personal relationships, an understanding of the unique personality of the child, and an appreciation of the human element in all learning situations. Self-education and professional insight merge as one unity in the growing self of the teacher. Free open discussion, in a strengthening climate, provides an opportunity for emotional release which frequently eventuates in broadened knowledge, in discovery of new classroom approaches to the individual child and to the group, and in modification of teachers' attitudes toward children, parents, and other teachers in the direction of seeing the other person as potentially positive and healthy even in the light of defeating threats and pressures.

In such an atmosphere the teacher arrives at satisfying perceptions and insights into educational concepts, issues, and dilemmas, grows as a unique personality, and discovers the value and meaning of a personal relationship in all significant human learning.

Date Due